UNIVERSITIES IN TRANSITION

UNIVERSITIES IN TRANSITION

H. C. DENT

COHEN & WEST

30 PERCY STREET · LONDON W. I

First Published 1961

© H. C. Dent 1961

Made and printed in England by
STAPLES PRINTERS LIMITED
at their Rochester, Kent, establishment

PREFACE

In offering this book to the public I wish to make clear that I do not pretend to be in any sense an authority on university affairs. I do not even claim to be able to write about them 'from the inside'. I have long been deeply interested in university education, and I have for the past four and a half years had the honour of being a member of the academic staff of the University of Sheffield. But that is my only first-hand experience, other than such as I have gained from brief visits, of the life and work of a university. So short a period would not, in my opinion, entitle anyone – unless he were exceptionally able, and devoted himself to the task with single-minded industry – to speak with authority about the elaborate and intricate complex of traditions, conventions, procedures, and mechanisms within which the British universities – each different from all the others – live and move and have their being. In my particular case there is far less justification for any such claim, because in my capacity as Director of the University's Institute of Education I have necessarily stood for the most part on the periphery, and not at the centre, of university life. I would ask, therefore, that the book be regarded as one written by what I believe the sociologists call a 'marginal man', that is, a person on the fringe of, but not completely involved in, the affairs and activities he surveys.

The book is addressed rather to the layman than to the academic. To many university teachers and administrators much of what I have written will be very familiar, though I hope that even they may find some points worth serious consideration. But today interest in university education is far from being confined to academic circles. It is widespread among the general public; especially, perhaps, among parents whose sons and daughters have recently attended, are now attending, or hope soon to enter, a university – in numerous instances as the first member of the family to do so. It is widespread, too, and far keener than ever before, among politicians, industrialists, business and professional men, and participants in local government. All these, I thought, might welcome a short account of the growth and development of universities in this country which paid particular attention to their present enormous expansion – a matter of critical importance to the nation's future.

The book is divided into three Parts: Past, Present, and Future. In Part I I have attempted to describe briefly what seem to me to have been some of the most significant developments in the long history of the English universities from their earliest days to the outbreak of the 1939–45 war. I have paid particular attention to the rise of the modern universities; first, because this is unquestionably by far the most important of all the developments in our university history since the emergence, some seven centuries previously, of Oxford and Cambridge, and secondly, because these universities, with others yet to be founded, may well dominate the future pattern of university education in England, and possibly throughout Great Britain.

In Part II I have tried to set down, in some detail, some parts of the story of post-war university expansion between 1945 and 1960, prefacing this with an outline survey of the wartime planning which made it possible to begin an ordered expansion almost immediately after hostilities had ceased. In Part III I have attempted to examine critically a few only – but I hope some of the most important – of the innumerable problems which have been thrown up, or rendered more serious, by the present expansion.

I should add that, apart from the one or two places where the University of Sheffield is mentioned by name, nothing written in this book has particular reference to that University. Nor, I trust, is any opinion expressed by me in these pages derived solely from, or even coloured largely by, my experiences at Sheffield. I have endeavoured throughout to see the picture as a whole.

Finally, while I am indebted to numerous people, and to a great variety of documentary information, I alone am responsible for the book's errors, defects and inadequacies.

I am indebted to the Controller of Her Majesty's Stationery Office for permission to quote extensively from official publications. My thanks are due also to the following: Ernest Benn, Ltd., for permission to quote from Professor W. H. G. Armytage's *Civic Universities* and Canon H. G. G. Herklots' *The New Universities*; the Clarendon Press for quotations from Hastings Rashdall's *The Universities of Europe in the Middle Ages* and Abraham Flexner's *Universities, American, English, German*; Faber and Faber, Ltd., for quotations from Bruce Truscot's *Redbrick University*; Methuen & Co., Ltd., for passages from Sir Charles Mallet's *History of the University of Oxford* and Sir Charles Grant Robertson's *The British Universities*; Routledge & Kegan Paul, Ltd., for quotations from José Ortega y Gasset's *Mission of the University*; the SCM Press, Ltd., for quotations from Sir Walter Moberly's *The Crisis in the University*; *Universities Quarterly* and Sir Eric Ashby for a quotation from an article by the latter.

I wish to express my thanks to Dr. A. W. Chapman, Registrar of the University of Sheffield, for putting at my disposal a collection of official and other documents, and to the Secretary of the University Grants Committee for supplying me with various statistics.

I wish to thank also my secretary, Mrs. Margaret Cuninghame-Green, for her typing of the manuscript, and for all the other assistance she gave me during the preparation of the book.

Whatlington, Sussex.   H. C. DENT.
November 30th, 1960.

CONTENTS

INTRODUCTION

The Universities of Europe stand beside the Empire and the Papacy among the most illustrious institutions which the genius of the Middle Ages shaped. They became powerful and privileged communities. They built up a great tradition. They made themselves the mouthpiece of mediaeval thought. But originally they were only guilds of teachers or of students, drawn together by the instinct of association which played so large a part in a disordered age. – SIR CHARLES MALLET.[1]

Universities, it can truly be said, have always been in transition. From the earliest days of those mediaeval gatherings of scholars out of which they grew they have never ceased to change. The process of change has been unending because the universities have never failed to respond to the pressures, both internal and external, which have continuously been brought to bear upon them. At some times they have responded willingly, at others reluctantly; at some times swiftly, at others very slowly; but sooner or later the response has always come. In the course of the centuries these responses have shaped and reshaped every element in the spirit, the life, and the work of universities: ideals, aims, and functions; government, finance and administration; subjects of study and academic standards; professional techniques and domestic life; relations with State and local authority, with the Church, with other educational institutions, and with society at large.

Even during the course of the Middle Ages the universities were transformed almost out of recognition, from rudimentary groups of teachers and learners into highly organised corporations, often not only mighty in scholarship but also powerful in politics. Few people would, I think, deny that as large a transformation has

[1] *A History of the University of Oxford*, Methuen, 1924, Vol. I., p. 25.

taken place in modern times. Yet it is still possible to claim that, despite all the changes which have taken place, the European university remains today essentially the same entity its creators conceived. 'There are', Sir Eric Ashby has written, 'profound differences between those turbulent societies of students in fourteenth-century Bologna and Paris and the prim "Redbrick" of the 1950s. But,' he adds, 'the similarities are even more profound.'[1]

Will that still be true in 2000 A.D.? Only the future can tell; but what seems already certain is that the transformation which the English universities are undergoing today may well prove as momentous as that which many centuries ago transformed itinerant bands of scholars into 'powerful and privileged communities' capable of making themselves 'the mouthpiece of mediaeval thought'.

In his attractive history of the University of Leicester[2] Professor Jack Simmons says that in the growth and development of universities in Europe there have been 'three great ages of expansion': in the twelfth and thirteenth centuries, when universities, as we understand them, came into being; in the fifteenth century, when some thirty more were founded [including, incidentally, three of the four in Scotland]; and during the past century and a half, when, to use Professor Simmons' words, 'universities have multiplied, and their scope has widened far beyond the conception of any earlier age'. It is my belief that, for England at any rate, that third age came to an end in 1939. The present expansion is different in kind from any which has preceded it, and should therefore be regarded as the opening stage of a fourth great age of expansion.

Because it is so different this new age may well prove as critical for the idea, the purpose, and the structure of the university as was the first, during which these were conceived and brought to birth. The range of possibilities seems to me to be very great. Without wishing to appear melodramatic I suggest that, on the one hand, the next few decades may witness the decay and death

[1] In *Technology and the Academics*, Macmillan, 1958, p. 2.
[2] *New University*, Leicester University Press, 1958.

of the idea of the university as a corporation of scholars united by a love of learning, and the consequent transformation of the university into an institution of higher education technically different, perhaps, from other such institutions, but spiritually in no way different: an institution, in fact, designed, staffed, and equipped to produce certain particular types of professionally trained specialists, and to do research of particular kinds in certain specified fields of knowledge. At the other extreme, these decades may equally well see the traditional idea of the university as a community of scholars once again vindicated. If that happens the university will remain, as it always has been hitherto, a unique institution, different in purpose and in character from any other. There are many people who would wish it so.

PART I

Past

CHAPTER ONE

I

As the darker ages passed away, and men's thoughts turned to learning once again, searching for a rule of right even in days of violent wrongdoing, searching for reasons to satisfy the doubter even in days when authority and dogma were supreme, the power of the teacher, never altogether lost, revived. Students gathered with strange enthusiasm, and if the records may be trusted, in surprising numbers, wherever famous teachers made a school, travelling up from lonely districts, voyaging from distant countries, amid the daily perils of mediaeval life. The chief of these resorts sprang into European fame. – SIR CHARLES MALLET.[1]

The first two centres of learning in Europe to take the shape of universities were both in Italy: at Salerno in the south and Bologna in the north. The former, which was well established, and highly reputed, by the middle of the eleventh century, was a school of medicine. The latter, which rose to fame in the early decades of the twelfth century, was a school of civil law. Neither of these subjects was to be found in the curricula of the cathedral and monastery schools, at that time almost the sole purveyors of education; hence the necessity to seek instruction in them elsewhere. The third university to emerge, at Paris about 1150–70, had a different origin; it grew out of the cathedral schools in the city, and attracted students by its teaching of philosophy and theology.

The fact that Salerno and Bologna were devoted exclusively to single fields of knowledge, and Paris in the first instance to no more than two, may serve to clear away at once a widespread misunderstanding about the function of a university. It is not, and

[1] Op. cit., Vol. I, p. 2.

never has been, to teach all subjects. A university is not, as has so often been incorrectly assumed, a place of universal knowledge. The word 'university' had, in fact, originally nothing whatever to do with subjects of study; it had to do with persons organised as a corporate body. It came to be attached to bodies of scholars because the students at Bologna (little is known about the organisation at Salerno), lacking the protective matrix of a cathedral or monastery, and being most of them strangers in a strange land, in an age when foreigners were by no means always welcome, and in any case were accorded no political or civic rights, felt impelled to band themselves together into a guild, or corporation, for mutual protection against robbery and violence, and in order to secure for themselves some corporate rights and privileges. There was nothing unusual in such action; all the skilled trades similarly banded themselves together for the same reasons. The current Latin term, used in all documents of incorporation, for any such guild or corporation, was *universitas vestra*, meaning simply 'all of you'.

Other universities followed the example of Bologna, and for some reason the name *universitas* became attached particularly to guilds of scholars. But it was not until the latter part of the fourteenth century that it was reserved exclusively to them. Before that, the term usually employed to designate a university was *studium generale*. Again, the name had at first no reference to the subjects taught. It had reference to the absence of restriction upon the localities whence students came. A *studium* was, quite simply, a place of study, a place where organised teaching and learning went on. (I avoid use of the word 'school', because today this invariably implies permanent buildings, whereas many *studia* had none.) If a *studium* became sufficiently well known and highly regarded to attract scholars from considerable distances it was referred to as a *studium universale*, or *studium commune*, or, most often, a *studium generale*.

At least, that was what happened in the case of the earliest universities. But it was not long after the emergence of Bologna and Paris (and Oxford in England) before there were many claimants to the title *studium generale*, some of them with but modest pretensions to higher learning; and consequently questions of status and of academic standards began to be matters of serious concern.

Bologna, and later Paris and Oxford, had become *studia generalia* by 'general recognition' (*ex consuetudine*, as the phrase was), that is, because scholars all over Christendom knew them to be places of learning of the highest rank. But early in the thirteenth century it began to be felt that certain conditions should be satisfied before the title of *studium generale* could be assumed: for example, that attendance should not be restricted to natives of any particular town or country; that the *studium* must teach not only the seven liberal arts but also at least one of the higher studies of law, medicine, and theology; and that it must have a sufficient, and sufficiently well qualified, staff. And it was felt that there must be some means of guaranteeing that such conditions were, in fact, satisfied.

The obvious means was the official sanction of an acknowledged public authority. By the end of the thirteenth century it had become accepted that the title of *studium generale* could be conferred upon an institution only by the Pope, the Emperor of the Holy Roman Empire, a king, or the municipal authority of a city republic. Even between these awards there was a crucial distinction; only the Pope and the Emperor had the power to confer upon a *studium generale* the right to grant the *ius ubique docendi*, that is, the right to grant degrees which entitled their holders, without further examination, to teach in any *studium generale*. Thus originated, six centuries ago, two conventions which, though modified in particulars, have in essence persisted to this day in the United Kingdom and many other countries. In our own country no university institution can be created save by Royal Charter, and the right to confer degrees is reserved exclusively to such chartered university institutions.

To earn the high distinction of being a Master of Arts, possessing the 'right to teach anywhere', the mediaeval student had to pursue a long and rigorous course of study, divided into two parts which together compassed all the seven liberal arts. These arts were arranged in two groups, the *Trivium* and the *Quadrivium*.

Starting normally at about the age of fourteen the student, who had previously acquired a working knowledge of Latin, the universal language of scholarship throughout Christendom, applied himself for three years (or longer) to the subjects of the *Trivium:* grammar (the Latin language and literature), logic, and rhetoric. At the end of this period, if he emerged successfully from the public 'disputations' (academic arguments on set topics) which were the mediaeval equivalent of external examinations, he became an 'incepting' (*i.e.*, commencing) Bachelor of Arts, and could go on to the four-year course of the *Quadrivium*. The subjects in this were called arithmetic, geometry, music, and astronomy – though it is perhaps hardly necessary to say that the subject matter under each of these heads was vastly different from that which goes under the same name today. At the end of this course the Bachelor had again to undergo the ordeal by disputation; if he survived he became an 'incepting' Master, eligible to receive the degree of Master of Arts and the 'right to teach anywhere'. If he wished then to specialise, he could embark upon a course, lasting eight years or longer, leading to a doctorate in canon law (*i.e.*, ecclesiastical law), civil law, medicine, or theology. But he was not allowed to undertake any of these specialised studies until he had successfully completed the general 'arts' course; that was obligatory upon all students.

The story of how systems of government developed at the universities of Bologna and Paris must be sought elsewhere. But one point of extreme importance must be mentioned here before restricting this narrative to the English universities. At Bologna it was the students – many of them grown men, and lawyers with established practices – who formed themselves into a *universitas* or, to be strictly accurate, into several *universitates*. Bologna, therefore, developed as a *universitas scholarium*, a corporation of students, which employed and paid its teachers – and incidentally reduced them to a sorry state of subjection. But at Paris it was the teachers who banded themselves together, and so Paris became a *universitas magistrorum* – a very different type of institution. Oxford, and all subsequent British universities, copied the Paris model. It is intriguing to try to imagine what our universities would be like today had Oxford copied Bologna; they would certainly be quite unlike what they are!

2

. . . there grew up at Oxford a great school or Studium, which acquired something of the fame of Paris and Bologna. – R. S. RAIT.[1]

It is customary, and proper, to begin the story of the British universities with the birth of a *studium generale* at Oxford during the latter half of the twelfth century. But it is, I think, essential to realise that this birth did not occur fortuitously. To continue the metaphor, not only had the child living parents, but a home had been prepared and was standing ready to receive it. Moreover, this child, which was later to grow into something unique, was not in its infancy much unlike other children that had previously been born into the same family. In other words, the emergence of a *studium generale* at Oxford, epoch-making though it was to prove, was at the time of its occurrence no more than a particular development in a tradition of scholarly learning which had persisted in Britain for many centuries.

That tradition had been sustained and expressed in three principal ways. First, in monasteries, where individual scholars or groups of scholars engaged in a rudimentary form of what we now call research, studying and transcribing the Scriptures, and writing commentaries and other learned works. The best known, and the most illustrious, example is the monastery at Jarrow during the time when it was adorned by the Venerable Bede, but monasteries at Canterbury, Glastonbury, and Lindisfarne – to name but three – had also produced work of scholarly distinction. Secondly, in the Grammar schools which were established as integral parts of all cathedral and collegiate churches. At their best these were very much more than 'schools' in the sense that we understand the

---

[1] *Life in the Medieval University*, Cambridge University Press, 1912, p. 6.

word today; they taught pupils of all ages, and covered in their curricula the greater part of the field of learning known to the Middle Ages. 'In the middle of the eighth century', wrote A. F. Leach many years ago, 'University and Grammar School were one';[1] and no one who has read Alcuin's famous, and oft-quoted, description of the programme of studies of the cathedral school at York under his predecessor Aethelbert (or Albert) can doubt the truth of that assertion.

> There he (Albert) moistened thirsty hearts with divers streams of teaching and varied dews of study; busily giving to some the arts of the science of grammar (*grammaticae rationis artes*), pouring into others the streams of the tongues of orators; these he polished on the whet-stone of law, those he taught to sing in Aeonian chant, making others play on the flute of Castaly, and run with the lyre over the hills of Parnassus. But others, the said master made to know the harmony of heaven and the sun, the labours of the moon, the five belts of the sky, the seven planets, the laws of the fixed stars, their rising and setting, the movements of the air and the sun, the earth's quake, the nature of men, cattle, birds and beasts, the different kinds of number and various (geometrical) figures: and he gave sure return to the festival of Easter; above all, revealing the mysteries of holy writ, for he opened the abysses of the old and rude law.[2]

Thirdly, a growth which arose apparently much later in time, there were the 'schools' which sprang up spontaneously in already established centres of learning when the fame of individual scholars of eminence drew thither students from distant parts, 'travelling up from lonely districts, voyaging from distant countries, amid the daily perils of mediaeval life', as Sir Charles Mallet put it. These spontaneous gatherings of scholars were the immediate progenitors of the earliest universities, for the 'daily perils' – by no means confined to travel – were among the strongest reasons which impelled scholars to form themselves into self-protective and self-assertive guilds, after the fashion of the times.

[1] In *The Schools of Mediaeval England*, Methuen, 1915, p. 59.
[2] Quoted from Leach, op. cit., pp. 58–9.

But the contributions made by the other two forms of organised learning and teaching to the idea of a university, as distinct from its organisation, should be neither overlooked nor underestimated, for they have remained among its essential elements. The monastic cell handed on the tradition and techniques of research, the Grammar school those of systematic teaching on a prescribed syllabus. Moreover, the Grammar school, relinquishing any claim to be itself a university, has continued to this day to carry out the indispensable task of giving youth that sound elementary training in the academic disciplines without which no one can confidently embark upon university studies.

Many examples of all these three forms of higher learning were to be found in England in the twelfth century – a period of great intellectual activity throughout Europe. Most numerous, probably, were the cathedral and collegiate schools, some of which, as my colleague Professor W. H. G. Armytage has recorded in his invaluable book *Civic Universities*[1] (to which I am most greatly indebted), had so broadened and deepened their curricula that they approached nearly to the mediaeval concept of a *studium generale*. Exeter, Lincoln, St. Paul's in London, Hereford, Salisbury, and York all possessed schools of this calibre. Why, then, it may be asked, did England's first University arise at Oxford rather than at one of these or other centres of learning?

Until further evidence than has as yet been unearthed becomes available – and so industrious have scholars been that the possibility seems remote – all discussion of this fascinating question must be more than a little speculative. The reason now generally accepted why the monastic and other schools which had existed at Oxford since the early decades of the twelfth century quite suddenly expanded, in or about 1167, into a *studium generale* is that this was a direct consequence of the quarrel between Henry II and his Archbishop, Thomas à Becket. As one of his moves in that quarrel, about 1167 (the exact year is uncertain) the King issued ordinances forbidding English clerics to travel to and from the Continent without his express permission, and ordering all those

[1] Benn, 1955. See pp. 31–4.

abroad who held benefices in England, and wished to retain them, to return home within three months. More or less coincidentally Louis VII of France, no friend of Henry II at any time, and currently supporting Becket, issued an edict expelling all alien scholars from France. As most of the English clerics in France at the time were students or teachers at the University of Paris, the result of these two royal commands was a considerable exodus – how large is disputed – of English scholars from France.

Now comes the interesting sequel. Once in England, a great many (though probably not all) of these scholars seem to have made direct for Oxford. Why there, rather than to any other of the well-known centres of learning ? So long as the evidence remains not entirely conclusive the temptation to speculate is almost overwhelming – and I shall not entirely resist it. But, first, the evidence, as adduced by recognised authorities. Oxford was readily accessible from all parts of the country, and no great distance from London, the capital. It was a flourishing market town, with good communications by road and river, and situated in a rich agricultural district; it could therefore be expected to be usually well stocked with supplies of food: no unimportant consideration in days when the threat of famine was never far distant. It was well known as a centre of learning; doubtless many of the immigrants had previously studied there. Finally, and perhaps decisively, it was a 'royal city', and not merely that, but one much beloved by the reigning monarch, who frequently resorted to his castle there. Consequently, a community of scholars lodged at Oxford might reasonably expect to enjoy the personal protection of a monarch known to be not only favourably disposed to learning but keenly aware of the practical advantages of having intellectuals at his side, and on his side.

It is at this point that I begin to speculate. The English clergy in general supported Henry in his quarrel with Becket, and Henry was far too astute a statesman to ignore the danger of losing their goodwill. The Paris scholars, all of whom were clerics, had been uprooted at his behest, and some of them, at least, might well be expected to resent having to move, and to harbour a grudge against the King for causing them to do so. Left to their own

initiative the immigrants would have had to make individual
arrangements for finding new places in which to teach and learn;
and this would undoubtedly have involved much breaking up of
schools and separation of friends. What more feasible than that
Henry, in some way or another, 'guided' the steps of the immigrants towards Oxford, indicating that here was a city where all
would find appropriate accommodation in congenial circumstances
– and where, incidentally, he could count henceforth upon a solid
phalanx of grateful, and valuable, adherents?

There is another possible speculation. Oxford was not a
cathedral city, and therefore not the seat of a bishop. Scholars at
Paris knew from experience how irksome to academic freedom a
bishop – who had absolute control over all forms of education –
could be. Did the thought of being remote from this over-riding
authority (the bishop's seat was at Lincoln) make Oxford seem yet
more attractive?

3

*. . . the habit of gregarious migration characteristic of medieval
scholars.* – HASTINGS RASHDALL.[1]

Though the scholars went to Oxford, that was no guarantee they
would remain there. Universities were in their early days
extremely insecure and unstable bodies. They were liable to be
suspended or closed down if they fell foul of high authority, be it
regal or ecclesiastical; they tended to disperse, at least temporarily
(they usually returned), when threatened by local peril or controversy; and they were perpetually subject to defections by dis-
gruntled teachers or students, or as the result of internal strife.
Migration, whether by the whole or part of a university, was easily
effected, because for long (in the case of Oxford for a century)

[1] *The Universities of Europe in the Middle Ages*, edited by F. M.
Powicke and A. B. Emden, Oxford University Press, 1936, Vol. III,
p. 30.

universities and their members owned little in the way of buildings or equipment.

All the foregoing eventualities except permanent closure occurred at Oxford. Among the many migrations three must be mentioned, because the first and third of these were followed by momentous consequences, and the second failed only by a narrow margin, and after a considerable period of time, to be equally important. In all three cases both royal and ecclesiastical authority played important parts; in two the former decided the issue. Independence of Church and State was far from being a characteristic of the early universities.

The first migration, in 1209, gave birth to the University of Cambridge. At Oxford a student killed a townswoman. He could not be found, so the town authorities arrested his fellow lodgers, and sought authority from the King to hang them. John, his country under interdict by Pope Innocent III, and himself either excommunicate or threatened with excommunication, was in no mood to make more enemies. He agreed. Two – possibly three – students were hanged. The University, filled with alarm, at once took flight, its members scattering far and wide. Some, it is said, returned to Paris; others went to nearby Reading, where there was a Cluniac abbey, to Canterbury, Maidstone, and – no one seems to know quite why – to Cambridge. There must, one imagines, have been schools there which attracted them, but if so history has left no record of them. All that is known is that there had long been in Cambridge an Augustinian priory, and that in the surrounding fens, at no great distance from the town, stood the great monasteries of Anglesey, Croyland, Ely, and Ramsey.

Except that some 'profane masters' are said to have remained, and to have 'irreverently lectured', there was no university in Oxford for five years. Then, King John having sought and received pardon from the Pope, the University returned in triumph. Its re-entry into the city was heralded by an Ordinance from the Pope's Legate which imposed drastic penalties upon the civic authorities for their part in the 1209 affray (and punishments upon the 'profane masters') and conferred upon the University rights and privileges which, with others acquired later, eventually made it the supreme authority in the borough.

The second great migration, in 1238, was the result of even more direct royal intervention. Again, a killing was the initial cause, but this time it was of a Papal Legate's brother, in an unseemly brawl between students and the Legate's servants which took place at the monastery at Oseney near Oxford, where the Legate was spending the night. The Legate, not unnaturally, protested to the King. Henry III responded by promptly suspending the University, which equally promptly packed up and left Oxford. Some of the scholars went to Salisbury and some to Northampton; and though most returned before very long, some remained. Had the wheel of fortune turned only slightly farther in favour of Northampton and Salisbury both of these cities might today be the homes of universities almost as ancient as Oxford and Cambridge.

There was at Salisbury a very famous school of theology. With the accession of the immigrants from Oxford this expanded into something approaching a *studium generale;* and this appears to have maintained itself for some forty years. After that it declined, though Salisbury remained for centuries a seat of learning, possessing two colleges, of which one may have had academic connections with Oxford.

The *studium* at Northampton had a somewhat shorter but more exciting life. Scholars from Cambridge joined the Oxford migrants, and, apparently with the encouragement and support of King Henry III, university studies proceeded steadily for nearly a quarter of a century. In 1261 there was a dramatic development. Following a serious disturbance at Cambridge, members of that university joined with Oxford migrants in petitioning the King to grant a licence for the foundation of a university at Northampton. Henry III at first listened favourably, but later changed his mind. Shortly after he was overwhelmed by the troubles which culminated in his defeat by Simon de Montfort at Lewes in 1265. This event was quickly followed by the abrupt termination of the life of the *studium generale* at Northampton. For Simon took serious heed of the complaint of the university and town of Oxford that their joint interests were being threatened by the continued existence of the Northampton *studium*, and, with the support of the ecclesiastical authorities of the day, ordered the teachers and scholars at Northampton, in the King's name, to return to Oxford. Some apparently refused, and were joined three years later by more scholars from Cambridge. But it was of no avail. Oxford, supported by both Church and State, was too powerful. Any chance of a University of Northampton was at an end.

The third, and the last, of the great migrations from Oxford was to Stamford in 1338. The cause of this was entirely different from those of the previous two, being the result of dissension within the University. In all the early universities there had grown up the practice for the scholars to group themselves together in 'Nations', according, usually, to the countries whence they came. At Oxford (and at Cambridge) there were two Nations, the Northerners (*Boreales*) and the Southerners (*Australes*), whose members came respectively from north or south of the river Trent. Frequent and furious fights took place between the Nations. It was one of these which, developing into a battle involving the town as well as the University, had prompted the Cambridge petition in 1261 for a University at Northampton. It was another which caused the Northerners at Oxford, worsted in a bloody strife, to secede to Stamford.

Universities in those days rarely hesitated to seek the aid of Church or State if they thought they would benefit thereby. In this case both sides appealed to the King. The Southerners, wiser in their generation, wrote on behalf of the University not only to the King, but also to the Queen and to the diocesan bishop of Lincoln. Edward III took their side decisively; he did not wish, he wrote, 'that schools or studies should be kept elsewhere within our realm except in the places where Universities are now in some sense held . . .'[1] And he forbade the holding of a university anywhere else. But the Northerners refused to budge, though the King repeated his orders, and sent the Sheriff of Lincoln to Stamford to proclaim them in person. Finally, some twelve

[1] Quoted from A. F. Leach, *Educational Charters and Documents 598 to 1909*, Cambridge University Press, 1911, p. 287.

months after their migration, the Northerners had to be evicted by force.

The incident had consequences of extreme importance not only for the universities but also for the country. As has been stated above, in his orders to the Stamford 'rebels' Edward III made it clear that he would allow in his kingdom no universities but those at Oxford and Cambridge. As soon as Stamford had been closed Oxford took steps to make this statement of royal policy effective. The University issued Ordinances making it compulsory from then on upon all its incepting Masters of Arts to swear a solemn oath that they would neither study nor lecture at Stamford, 'as in a university, seat of learning, or general college'.

Tu iurabis quod non leges nec audies Stamfordiae tanquam in universitate studio aut collegio generali.[1]

And 'so', says Professor Armytage, 'the door was finally closed on any further foundations of a university character outside Oxford and Cambridge'. It remained closed for nearly 500 years. Incredible though it may seem, Oxford continued to exact this oath from all its Masters until 1827. And, though several serious attempts were made, notably in the seventeenth century, to found other universities, and a number of institutions, including the Gresham College in London, established in 1596, and some at least of the eighteenth century Dissenting Academies, conducted studies at university level, no institution received a charter conferring upon it university status until 1829.

Whether or not this long-enduring Oxbridge monopoly was to the country's benefit is disputed. Professor Armytage thinks it was:[2]

Thus, by the concentration of academic energies, England avoided the dilution which characterised other countries, and as a result Oxford and Cambridge established a tradition for national as opposed to regional scholarship which has only recently been challenged.

[1] Quoted from Mallet, op. cit., Vol. I, p. 157 n.
[2] Op. cit., p. 45.

Dean Hastings Rashdall, in his monumental work on the mediaeval universities,[2] took a precisely opposite view:

> It is impossible to doubt that the cause of learning in England has been injured by the paucity of its universities, or that the stagnation of Oxford and Cambridge at certain periods of their history has been aggravated by the total absence of competition.[1]

Where the authorities differ so violently I would not dare to venture an opinion. What is, however, incontrovertible is that the centuries of monopoly enabled Oxford and Cambridge to acquire such eminence and esteem as to render it virtually impossible for the emerging university institutions of the nineteenth century to be regarded as even potentially their equals, in status or in scholarship. And, though the nineteenth century university colleges have now all achieved, on their merits, full university rank, this problem remains with us still, some people think in an even more acutely difficult form than in the nineteenth century.

[1] Op. cit., Vol. III, p. 90.

CHAPTER TWO

Two great movements mark the medieval history of the University – the struggle for independence and the rise of Colleges. – T. R. GLOVER.[1]

Professor Glover was writing about Cambridge, but his words are equally applicable to Oxford. Indeed, rather more so, for, as he admits, 'Cambridge . . . was slower in achieving its freedom'. So it was also in founding colleges. It was Oxford which took the lead in both the 'struggle for independence' and the creation of the collegiate system.

If a precise date can ever justifiably be suggested as marking the conclusion of a stage in a process of continuous growth, it can be said that 1338 marked the end of the period of instability and insecurity for Oxford and Cambridge. This is not to say that they had no troubles to come. But from 1338 their position as national institutions could be regarded as assured; and, as has been noted, their sole right to that position remained unassailable for half a millennium, despite the periods of 'stagnation' to which Dean Rashdall refers.

There was, of course, no abrupt transition from instability to stability. The forces making for stability, security, and assurance had, in fact, been operating ever since the earliest days of the *studium generale* at Oxford, if not before. As has been suggested, there might never have been a university at Oxford had not Henry II recalled the English scholars from Paris. And it is clear, I hope, from even the brief outline of selected incidents in the early life of Oxford which I have given that throughout the period they cover the University owed much to royal support and encouragement; on occasions, indeed, owed to this its continued

[1] *Cambridge Retrospect*, Cambridge University Press, 1943. p. 9.

existence. The same is true of Cambridge, though to a lesser degree, because until towards the end of the fourteenth century this University did not begin to rival Oxford in reputation, and so attracted less attention in high places.

Independence from royal authority was not attempted during this first period; on the contrary, Oxford seems to have had every inclination to shelter under the royal wing. What was quickly attempted, and steadily secured, was independence of the local authority. The Papal Legate's ordinance of 1214 marked the first large step in this direction; it contained a clause which provided that any cleric arrested by the town authorities had to be at once surrendered 'on the demand of "the Bishop of Lincoln, or the Archdeacon of the place or his Official, or the Chancellor [the head of the University], or whomsoever the Bishop of Lincoln shall depute to this office".'[1] Though this ordinance did not actually alter the previous constitutional position, it was extremely important from the University's point of view. It gave to the Chancellor a share in an authority enjoyed up to that time exclusively by the Bishop of the diocese, in whom was vested supreme control over all organised education.

Thanks to frequent support from both the monarch and the ecclesiastical authorities the University was able to wrest privilege after privilege from the town. In 1231 the King compelled the town authorities to allow the Chancellor the use of their prison for confining delinquent clerics. From 1248 the town mayor and bailiffs, on assuming office, had to swear on oath to respect the customs and liberties of the university. In 1275 further rights in handling disputes between the University and the town were granted to the Chancellor, and scholars' hostels were deemed immune from various civic liabilities. In 1355 there came what may be called the grand climax. A tremendous battle, lasting several days, took place between townsmen and students. The King intervened, and deprived town and university alike of their charters. But whereas the members of the University were granted a general pardon, the town authorities were compelled to sur-

[1] Rashdall, op. cit., Vol. III, p. 37.

render to the Chancellor a long list of cherished municipal rights. 'From this time forward', wrote Rashdall,[1] 'the town of Oxford was practically governed by the University'.

The story of the relationships between the mediaeval University and the Church is far more complicated. It is, so to speak, a story within a story, for in the Middle Ages all education was the province of the Church, and the University, as an educational institution, was implicitly assumed to be under ecclesiastical control. Every teacher had to be licensed by the diocesan bishop, and every student was a cleric – though not necessarily in orders – and therefore subject to ecclesiastical discipline.

The organisation of both Oxford and Cambridge was modelled upon that of Paris, which, as has been said, grew out of the cathedral schools in that city. The head of each university was the Chancellor (*Cancellarius*), who was a cathedral officer, appointed by and responsible to the diocesan Bishop. As such, he had no power to act independently. But at Oxford (contrary to Paris) the Chancellor seems from very early days to have achieved some measure of independence. This may well have been because Oxford was not only not a cathedral city, but was also at a considerable distance from the bishop's seat at Lincoln. It also appears that for some of the time during the latter half of the twelfth century the episcopal chair was vacant.

In short, the Chancellor was on the spot, while the Bishop was not. It is easy to imagine that the Bishop tended to rely more and more on his representative, while the Chancellor tended increasingly to identify himself with his university colleagues rather than with the Bishop. Similarly, these would tend more and more to regard him as one of themselves rather than as the Bishop's officer. So it is not surprising to find them before long claiming the right to have their nominee appointed to the office.

The Chancellor's rise to a position of independent power and responsibility was greatly facilitated by the appointment in 1235 of Robert Grosseteste as Bishop of Lincoln. For Grosseteste went to the episcopal chair direct from the Chancellorship of Oxford,

[1] Op. cit., p. 100.

of which he was the first known holder. He was, moreover, one of the most distinguished scholars of the day, a man of highly original mind with wide interests, and an outstandingly good administrator. He had great influence both at the Court and in the Church: and so he was able to prove as valuable as he was devoted to his University. He got it out of a very serious conflict with the King in 1255 more successfully than probably anyone else could have done; and Rashdall has recorded[1] that 'so long as the See of Lincoln was filled by Robert Grosseteste almost unbroken harmony prevailed between the university and the diocesan'.

Unhappily, that state of affairs did not persist; for almost a century after Grosseteste's episcopacy there were recurrent disputes between the University and the bishop. Throughout this period the University steadily improved its position, and later it did so vis à vis the Archbishop of Canterbury, a much more formidable authority than the diocesan. The latter success was secured only after what appeared at the time a most humiliating defeat: the occasion, in 1382, when the Archbishop compelled the Chancellor to come to London, and there to kneel humbly before him and beg his pardon because the University had disobeyed his order to condemn officially the heresies of John Wyclif. The Archbishop's triumph was complete, for he not only humiliated the Chancellor but compelled the retirement of Wyclif and many of his followers from the University, thus depriving it of much of its intellectual vigour and most of the courage which had made it the nation's spokesman in protesting against ecclesiastical abuses. Yet only thirteen years later the University secured from Pope Boniface IX a Bull exempting it from the jurisdiction of all archbishops and bishops, and entrusting to the Chancellor complete power to deal with all offences committed by members of the university. True, in 1411 this Bull was revoked, but nevertheless 'the liberty which Arundel [the Archbishop] had struck at did not disappear.'[2]

The third force making for stability at Oxford and Cambridge

[1] Op. cit., p. 115.
[2] Mallet, op. cit., Vol. I, p. 239.

was one which was ultimately to render these universities unique in the world: the growth of the collegiate system. This growth began to take shape at Oxford about the middle of the thirteenth century, but like all processes of growth it had its origins long before. From the earliest days of the University groups of students had been in the habit of renting jointly houses in which to live together – a practice they may have learned from Paris, where it was usual. Common sense probably suggested the idea that one of their number should be made responsible for the rent and administration of the house – though again this arrangement was frequent in Paris. As the University grew in strength it began to feel concern about these hostels. On the one hand it desired that they should be under responsible control, and preferably that a Master should be in charge; on the other it wanted to ensure that the occupants were not charged too high rents, a malpractice from which the thirteenth century Oxford townsfolk were no more immune than any other landlords anywhere. In 1231 a royal order was secured which provided that all hostel rents should be determined by a joint committee of two Masters of Arts and two responsible citizens.

Parallel with these developments went another. Many students were very poor; and this began to move benefactors to bequeath or donate sums of money towards their maintenance – a clear sign, incidentally, that the universities were coming to be not only known but respected and valued. Two Oxford colleges, University and Balliol, were to grow out of such endowment of hostels; and so to be able to claim the honour of being the first among the college foundations. In 1249 William of Durham, believed to have been rector of Wearmouth, left 310 marks for the maintenance of ten or more Masters of Arts who were studying theology. The University spent part of the money on buying houses. In 1260, Sir John de Balliol (grandfather of the Balliol who contested the Scottish crown with Robert Bruce), having to make penance for offences against the Church, gave money to maintain a group of poor scholars at Oxford.

But in their early days neither Durham Hall nor Balliol Hall were colleges. The essential element was lacking. Like the word *universitas*, the word *collegium* had originally nothing to do with buildings; it had to do with persons organised as a legal corporation. It was Walter de Merton, a former Chancellor of England, who in 1264 introduced this element; and it is significant that he did not, in the original statutes which he drew up for the 'House of the Scholars of Merton', provide a residence for them. What he did was to donate the revenues of two manors in Surrey:

> . . . for the perpetual maintenance of 20 scholars living in the schools at Oxford, or elsewhere where a University may happen to flourish, and for the maintenance of two or three ministers of the altar of Christ living in the said house; on the condition and in the matter underwritten . . . [1]

It is also significant that Merton did not originally require that his scholars should necessarily study at Oxford – strong evidence that even in 1264 the University was not regarded as being permanently located there. It was not until ten years later that he provided for them a residence at Oxford – and he had previously purchased a house at Cambridge, presumably in case it became advisable for the scholars to move there. What he did, and kept on doing – for he revised and amplified his statutes in 1270 and again in 1274 – was to provide for his scholars a permanent endowment, to lay down conditions of admission to the community and regulations for their life and study together, and to embody all these provisions in a legal document of incorporation

In this he specified that his scholars were each to receiv annually at least 40s. sterling, to live together in the house, and wear uniform. They were to be members of his family, but, if there were not enough of these who were judged 'upright and able and desirous of proficiency', the number was to be made up from 'other honest and able persons, especially from the diocese of Winchester'.

But the scholars were only to receive their maintenance so long as they behaved themselves 'well and like gentlemen', and they

[1] Quoted from A. F. Leach, *Educational Charters and Documents 598 to 1909*, p. 171.

could be deprived of it, not only if they failed to do so, but also for a variety of other reasons.

> if any of them yield to fate, or take the religious habit, or transfer themselves to other duties, obtain better benefices, depart from the University, or refuse to apply themselves to study after their capacity, are publicly defamed of anything disgraceful, or otherwise behave themselves badly or in an ungentlemanly way . . .

To ensure good management and good discipline there was to be a Warden in charge of the House. He was to be nominated by the twelve senior scholars, who were to be advised by the 'brethren', and the nominators were urged to 'endeavour to nominate . . . the best and most faithful administrator of the property and business of the house'.

The subjects which the scholars were to study were prescribed: arts, philosophy, canon law or theology; 'and the greater part of them shall devote themselves to the study of the liberal arts and philosophy, until at the will of the warden and fellows, as being persons laudably proficient in them, they transfer themselves to the study of theology'.[1]

Merton's intention in founding his House was quite specific; it was to provide a steady and regular supply of scholars who would become 'seculars', that is, parish priests. They were not to become 'regulars'; if they did 'take the religious habit', that is, enter an order of monks or friars, they had to leave the House.

Merton may have got his idea from Paris, where the College of the Sorbonne had been founded in 1257 to provide for students of theology. Be that as it may, he set a fashion in England which was quickly copied and universally adopted. His revised and amplified foundation deed of 1274 became the model upon which were based the statutes of almost all the many colleges founded in Oxford and Cambridge during the Middle Ages. Within a century there were a dozen or more of these. The first at Cambridge, Peterhouse, was founded in 1284 by Hugh de Balsham, Bishop of

---

[1] Quotations from Leach, op. cit., pp. 173, 177, 183.

Ely, whose statutes expressly provided that its members should 'in everything live together as students at Oxford who are called of Merton'. By 1350 Gloucester Hall (later Worcester College), Exeter, Oriel, and Queen's had been added to Balliol, University, and Merton at Oxford, while at Cambridge Clare, Pembroke, Gonville (later Gonville and Caius), and King's Hall and Michael-house, which were later to be merged in Trinity, had taken their places alongside Peterhouse.

It must not be supposed that the establishment of colleges transformed rapidly the life, work and discipline at Oxford and Cambridge – though it should not be overlooked that, in Professor Armytage's words, 'from . . . 1274 Merton College became the dominant community in the intellectual life of Oxford'.[1] There were two main reasons why for long the impact of the colleges upon the universities was slight. First, the numbers of collegiate scholars were relatively very small;[2] and secondly, for a century or more they provided only for scholars who had already gradu-ated. It was not until the foundation in 1379 of New College, Oxford, by William of Wykeham, Bishop of Winchester, that undergraduates began to be provided for on any scale – in that case by founding a school, Winchester College, to supply the young scholars.

The founding of colleges went on steadily throughout the fourteenth and fifteenth centuries, and as the number of colleges grew, so did their influence; in fact, there was to come a time when the Universities of Oxford and Cambridge were to be little more than collections of independent and powerful colleges, self-governing, self-supporting, and self-replenishing.

[1] Op. cit., p. 42.
[2] Not more than seventy-three at Oxford in 1350, it has been estimated: see S. C. Roberts, *British Universities*, Collins, 1947. p. 13.

CHAPTER THREE

. . . all this busy ferment of new knowledge and education . . . –
W. H. G. ARMYTAGE.[1]

'The ecclesiastical repression which followed the collapse of the
Wyclifite heresy,' wrote Rashdall,[2] 'meant the extinction of all
vigorous and earnest scholastic thought' at Oxford. 'The great
realist and nominalist debate lingered on for a century more; but
all the life had been taken out of it: all real, fresh, intellectual
activity was beginning to divert itself into other channels'. The
Renaissance and the Reformation were at hand, when, in Rashdall's words, 'the human mind rose in rebellion' against 'an
effete traditionalism'. In England it was Cambridge rather than
Oxford which led that rebellion.

Never did the light of Cambridge shine more brightly than
during the sixteenth century, when it was, in Professor Glover's
words, 'the very centre and heart of the Reformation movement'.
Tyndale, Coverdale, Latimer, Ridley, and Cranmer were among
the men who made it this. But Cambridge has claims also to be
regarded as the 'centre and heart' of the English Renaissance.
While Oxford remained hesitant about the value of Greek (it was
later to make noble amends) Cambridge invited the great
Erasmus, the most renowned scholar in western Europe, to be its
first teacher of the subject. It was Cardinal John Fisher, of whom
it has been said that 'perhaps at no other time has the University
owed so much, for so long, to one man',[3] who induced Erasmus to
come. He at the same time persuaded Lady Margaret Beaufort
(mother of Henry VII) to found two new colleges at Cambridge,

---

[1] *Civic Universities*, p. 84.   [2] Op. cit., pp. 270 and 271.
[3] H. C. Porter, *Reformation and Reaction in Tudor Cambridge*,
C.U.P., p.3.

Christ's and St. John's, which only fifteen years later Erasmus judged among the three colleges that were foremost in the new learning. At the third, Queen's, he had himself worked, teaching Greek and preparing an edition of the New Testament in Greek which was to become both famous and influential throughout Europe.

Not only scholarship but politics also was to enliven the sixteenth century scene at the Universities. 'I judge no land in England better bestowed than that which is given to our universities', said King Henry VIII in an oft-quoted remark. But not that part of it bestowed upon the Church. In 1547 commissioners sent by his minister Thomas Cromwell swept away all ecclesiastical endowments and monastic foundations at Oxford and Cambridge. In compensation the King founded at each University Regius professorships of Divinity, Greek, Hebrew, Civil Law, and Physic (medicine). At Oxford he refounded the great college which Cardinal Wolsey had built and renamed it Christ Church, and at Cambridge he united King's Hall, Michaelhouse and other halls in the magnificent college of Trinity.

But the expropriation of ecclesiastical funds and property had one disastrous effect, which it is to be hoped was not foreseen by those who planned and carried it out. The 'poor and indigent' scholars who had been the mainstay of the mediaeval universities were no longer able to come in such numbers as previously, for the cheap maintenance they had found in the monastic hostels was no longer available. As early as 1549 Hugh Latimer was complaining to Henry's son, the young King Edward VI, that 'there be none now but great men's sons in colleges'. The day had begun of the 'gentleman commoner', who paid for his own tuition and lodging, and by his wealth sent up the cost of living at the University. From this time on the universities became increasingly a 'class preserve', inhabited ever more largely by the sons of rich men and aristocrats. The new statutes framed for both Universities in 1549 also gave a controversial colour to the curricula, which were designed to encourage Protestantism and eliminate Roman Catholicism. The era of religious tests had opened; it was to endure for over three centuries.

In 1564 Queen Elizabeth came to Cambridge, riding on her palfrey, so it is recorded, into the hall of St. John's College, and in 1570 she gave to that university yet another new set of statutes. These greatly increased the power of the heads of colleges, and thus, in Professor Glover's words,[1] 'transformed the ancient democracy into an oligarchic government'. He quotes a contemporary as saying (no doubt with some exaggeration) that the college heads

> keepe Benefices and be non-residentes. While they are clothed in scarlet, their flocks perish for cold; and while they fare deliciouslie, their people are faint with a most miserable hunger.

As had happened before, no sooner had the Universities attained a position of apparent security and eminence than forces internal and external began to undermine it. Throughout the sixteenth century Oxford and Cambridge grew in power and esteem. Schools – Harrow, Merchant Taylors', Rugby, Shrewsbury, and Westminster were among them – were founded to supply them with the right type of student, that is, the well-born student who might later be expected to occupy a responsible post in the service of Church or State. In 1603 James I confirmed the national importance of the Universities by granting them the right to be represented in Parliament, a right they were to retain for nearly 350 years.

But long before that, forces had begun to operate which were to diminish this importance, and to lead in the seventeenth century to the Universities' monopoly of higher education being seriously challenged. One of the causes of decline was the Universities' inability to adapt their curricula to emerging social needs. Long previously the clergy – and the university teachers were all clergy – had been forbidden to teach civil law. Consequently, law schools had been established in London. Adopting the collegiate system, they had built up four 'Inns of Court', of which by the mid-sixteenth century one at least, Lincoln's Inn, was larger than any college in Oxford or Cambridge. To the Inns of Court flocked

[1] Op. cit., p. 22.

the scions of the aristocracy; and so one of the two professions which called the European university into being drew apart from it in England, never to be completely re-united.

Similarly, despite Henry VIII's Regius Professorships, and many instances of valuable experimental work at the Universities, medicine, the other profession most anciently linked with university education, also began to draw away, forming its own associations. At the same time various continental universities built up distinguished schools of medicine to which went many English scholars.

Two centuries previously Oxford had begun to lose one valuable group of students. Balliol College, founded by a Scot, had in its early days been filled predominantly with Scottish students. But the campaigns of Edward I and II and the achievement of Scottish independence by Robert Bruce, had diverted these to Paris – there being no universities in their own country. When, in the early years of the fifteenth century, Paris became virtually closed to them, because of the 'Great Schism' with its rival Popes at Rome and Avignon, they did not return to Oxford, but made for St. Andrews in Fife; and there, thanks to the Bishop, Henry Wardlaw, Scotland's first university was born in 1411. So great was the joy at this happy event that the arrival of the Papal Bull confirming the University Charter was celebrated by two whole days of continuous merrymaking. Forty years later the University of Glasgow was founded, and in 1494 the University of Aberdeen – both also on episcopal initiative. Nearly a century was to elapse before Edinburgh University was created in 1583 by the town council; but before the end of the sixteenth century Scotland, a poverty-stricken country with a far smaller population than England, possessed double the number of universities its wealthier neighbour had. Small and struggling though these universities were for a long time, they nourished, and enhanced, the tradition of scholarly learning, especially in philosophy and theology, which had been born centuries before in Scotland, and never wholly lost.

The seventeenth century was full of trouble for both Oxford and Cambridge. From its start they had many critics, some of whom proposed their abolition, and many alternative institutions were projected, of which a few were actually established.

Francis Bacon complained that the universities, of Europe as well as England, neglected the sciences and 'matters mechanical', and sketched in his *New Atlantis* (1627) a Solomon's House, to be devoted to 'the knowledge of Causes, and . . . the effecting of all things'. In 1635 Sir Francis Kynaston established, with the approval and financial support of Royalty, a 'Museum Minervae' which, had it succeeded, might have become the prototype of an English technological university, for it opened with professors of astronomy, fencing, geometry, languages, medicine, and music. But the universities killed it – or so Samuel Hartlib said.

James I had previously launched his own project, a theological college intended to be, in Thomas Fuller's words,[1] 'a spiritual garrison . . . where learned divines should study and write in maintenance of all controversies against the Papists'. Chelsea College got as far as a Royal Charter and what we should call today the 'first phase' in its building programme. It also counted among its Fellows during its brief existence William Camden the antiquarian, Thomas Heywood the dramatist, Robert Abbot, who subsequently became Regius Professor of Divinity at Oxford, and John Overall, an erudite theologian who later was a bishop three times over.

Among schemes which look more practicable to modern eyes were the proposals to found universities at Ripon in Yorkshire, Carlisle, Manchester, Shrewsbury, and Durham. The first received an endowment from the king, out of previously confiscated funds, but the result was a collegiate church (now the cathedral), and not a university. The petition on behalf of Carlisle, made in 1617, was rejected by James I, and Shrewsbury never got beyond proposals. The Manchester project was a casualty of the Civil War, and Durham (which was almost brought to birth) of the Restoration.

Oxford's strong support of Charles I – Archbishop Laud, an Oxonian, had filled the Fellowships of the Colleges with his

[1] *Church History* (ed. J. S. Brewer, Oxford, 1845, V, 387). Quoted from Armytage, op. cit., p. 97.

nominees – as early as 1643 provoked proposals in Parliament
(from members of the university) that a university be established
in London, the centre of the Parliamentary cause. Hartlib supported the idea enthusiastically. John Milton went farther; he
wanted colleges set up in every city. Among other projects mooted
at this time were rural colleges, a teachers' training college, a
college of husbandry, and a technical college for artisans. None
came to anything.

Nor did any of the proposals for abolishing, or at the least dis-
endowing, Oxford and Cambridge. The Universities not only
weathered the gale of antagonism, undoubtedly the stiffest they
had encountered, but beat off all would-be marauders, and sailed
serenely into port at the Restoration. But it is perhaps no
exaggeration to say that, for a century thereafter, they were
done more harm by patronage and protection than they had
suffered previously from hostility. It were perhaps kindest to
draw the veil completely over the story of Oxford and Cambridge
from 1660 to the end of the eighteenth century. But that cannot
justifiably be done; all one can do is to make the story mercifully
brief.

The Act of Uniformity passed in 1662 restricted membership
of the English universities to members of the Established Church.
It was followed by other Acts of the same kind. All teachers who
would not take the required oaths were expelled; they included
thirteen Oxford and six Cambridge heads of Colleges, and
seventy-five Fellows. As a result student numbers fell, and
discipline deteriorated. 'The dons neglected their duties, and
their pupils did not fall short of so engaging an example'.[1]

In 1660 a new type of challenge was presented to Oxford and
Cambridge. Following up suggestions made by John Evelyn, the
diarist, and others, some forty men of learning who were particularly interested in science agreed to hold regular meetings together in London. Two years later the group became incorporated
as the Royal Society. Despite the opposition of the Universities
this had from the start an irresistible attraction for eminent

---

[1] Glover, op. cit., p. 32.

scholars; and, profiting largely from the University expulsions, the Royal Society quickly became the national centre of scientific experiment and research.

From 1675 another challenge, again of a different kind, began to confront the Universities. In that year Charles Morton, an Oxford graduate, opened at Stoke Newington in London the first of the 'Dissenting Academies'. His example was quickly copied all over the country: at places so far apart as Lincoln and Taunton, Sheffield and Saffron Walden, Whitehaven and Ipswich, as well as in London. Staffed in their earlier days largely by teachers who had been expelled from Oxford and Cambridge, the Academies at their best gave an education of university quality, often in a wider range of subjects and in a manner better calculated to serve the needs of the age; and, above all, to everyone who cared to attend, irrespective of religious affiliations. Despite continuous attacks upon them, including an Act of Parliament, the Schism Act, 1714, designed expressly to destroy them, they maintained themselves until the early days of the nineteenth century, when, having served their purpose, of opening more widely the gates to university education, they faded away, having blazed the trail for the universities and colleges of the nineteenth century.

Meanwhile Oxford and Cambridge sank ever deeper into sloth and social frivolities. Not all dons, it is true, deserved Edward Gibbon's ferocious condemnation, nor were all students drinkers, gamblers, and worse, as Cowper said most of them were in his time. But the volume of criticism, from persons who had had personal experience, is too large and too uniform to be discounted. It may be summed up in two quotations, one from Adam Smith and one from Wordsworth.

In the universities the youth neither are taught, nor always can find any proper means of being taught, the sciences which it is the business of those incorporated bodies to teach.[1]

Wordsworth put it in kindlier but no less devastating fashion, in the *Prelude*:

[1] *The Wealth of Nations*, Routledge, 1890, p. 601.

> *We sauntered, played, or rioted; we talked*
> *Unprofitable talk at morning hours,*
> *Drifted about along the streets and walks,*
> *Read lazily in trivial books, went forth*
> *To gallop through the country in blind zeal*
> *Of senseless horsemanship, or on the breast*
> *Of Cam sailed boisterously, and let the stars*
> *Come forth, perhaps without one quiet thought.*

CHAPTER FOUR

Why universities and colleges should only be at Oxford and Cambridge, I know no reason . . . It would be more advantageous to the good of all the people, to have universities or colleges, one at least at every great town in the nation, as in London, York, Essex, Bristol, Exeter, Norwich and the like; and for the State to allow to these Colleges competent maintenance for some godly and learned men to teach. –
WILLIAM DELL.[1]

The opinion of the seventeenth century Master of Gonville and Caius College, Cambridge, was to be echoed many times, but more than a century and a half was to elapse before the vision he saw began to be translated into reality; and yet another century and a half before, in our own days, it came to anything approaching full fruition.

The idea of a University in London was mooted at intervals from the fifteenth century onwards. But it was not until 1825 that effective action was taken. On February 9th of that year a letter appeared in *The Times*, written by the poet Thomas Campbell, who proposed:

a great London university . . . an institution for effectively and multifariously teaching, examining, exercising and rewarding with honours in the liberal arts and sciences the youth of our middling rich people between the ages of fifteen or sixteen and twenty or later . . . a university combining the advantages of public and private education, the emulative spirit produced by examination before numbers and by honours conferred before

[1] *The Right Reformation of Learning, Schools and Universities.* Pamphlet written in 1653, quoted by Armytage, *Civic Universities*, p. 110.

45

the public, the cheapness of domestic residence, and all the moral influences that result from home.

No one could have imagined at the time what a strange and troubled institution was to result from that proposal.

The story of the beginnings of London University has been told so often that there is no need to do more here than recapitulate it in brief outline. A group of influential Dissenters, including Henry, Lord Brougham – to the fore in all projects for educational reform – George Birkbeck, the pioneer of Mechanics Institutes, Jeremy Bentham, James Mill, and Thomas Campbell, in 1828 opened in Gower Street 'London University' to provide for students excluded from the ancient universities by reason of their religious affiliations a sound and cheap university education. An equally, if not more influential, group of Anglicans, including the Duke of Wellington, shocked at the impiety of a 'godless' institution which imposed no religious tests for admission, opened in 1831, in the Strand, King's College, to make available an even sounder university education, because it would include 'a knowledge of the doctrines and duties of Christianity' as inculcated by the United Church of Great Britain and Ireland. Neither institution succeeded in securing the coveted university charter. King's College was granted a university college charter, but this did not give it the power to grant degrees, and it refused to combine with the 'University of London' for that purpose. After long but fruitless discussions the Government created in 1836 a separate University of London with no teaching function. It was purely an examining body, but it had power to affiliate colleges which fulfilled the requirements it laid down, and to grant degrees to their students. King's College and 'London University', now renamed University College, London, became the first two affiliated colleges.

Within fifteen years London University had affiliated nearly ninety colleges. In 1858 its degrees were thrown open to non-collegiate students as well, that is, to anyone possessing sufficient ability to pass its examinations and sufficient ready money to pay its examination fees. This breathtaking contraction of the meaning of the term 'university' was later, by one of the strangest ironies of educational history, to produce most beneficial consequences, to which reference will be made later. At this juncture I am concerned to emphasise one point only: that the foundation of London University as an examining body only was not the result of a deliberate attempt to create a new conception of university education. It was simply an attempt to solve otherwise intractable religious and social problems: the exclusion of Dissenters from Oxford and Cambridge, and the high cost of education at those universities. London cannot therefore be regarded as the prototype of the *modern* university, expressly planned to foresee, and satisfy, the needs of a society which was being rapidly transformed from an agricultural to an industrial one. Some of its affiliated institutions were so planned, but the university itself was for many decades stunted in its development by the limitations forced upon it by the circumstances of its foundation. But it did at least break the long Oxbridge monopoly.

The creators of the University of Durham, which was founded four years before London, did not pretend to look forward. They quite frankly looked to the past; for they modelled their creation upon Oxford, and linked it closely with the cathedral, out of whose accumulated wealth the foundation was largely financed.

The task of facing the future was undertaken during the second half of the nineteenth century by a combination of enlightened private enterprise and civic pride. The story of the rise of the civic universities has been so fully and admirably told by Professor Armytage that, as in the case of London University, I feel I can safely cut the strictly chronological matter to a minimum. What I want rather to do is to underline certain crucially important aspects of the growth and development of these universities which I believe to have particular significance for the future of university education in Great Britain.

The colleges founded in England and Wales during the nineteenth century which are the direct ancestors of present-day universities are as follows:

ENGLAND

Owens College, Manchester	1851
Hartley Institution, Southampton	1850
	(opened 1862)
Newcastle College of Physical Science, Newcastle-upon-Tyne	1871
Yorkshire College of Science, Leeds	1874
College of Science for the West of England, Bristol	1876
Firth College, Sheffield	1879
Mason Science College, Birmingham	1880
University College, Nottingham	1881
University College, Liverpool	1881
University Extension College, Reading	1892
Exeter Technical and University Extension College, Exeter	1895

WALES

University College, Aberystwyth	1872
University College, Cardiff	1883
University College, Bangor	1884

Many of these institutions passed through one or more metamorphoses, chiefly by amalgamation, before they attained university status. One large group of amalgamations in particular should receive special mention: with earlier established medical schools. This happened in the nineteenth century at Birmingham, Bristol, Leeds, Liverpool, Manchester, and Sheffield, and was also to happen later at London and in Wales.

These amalgamations with medical schools are mentioned particularly, first, because of the extensive scale on which they took place, and secondly, because they help to show that the statement frequently made, and still accepted by many people, that the modern universities were created largely for the purpose of teaching science and technology is far from being wholly correct. This belief is epitomized in the following quotation:[1]

[1] H. G. G. Herklots, *The New Universities*, Benn, 1928, p. 26. This quotation is used solely by way of illustration.

> The modern universities are largely the creations of industrial-
> ism. They were created by industrialism to meet her own
> needs. Science came first. Art found her way in later.

The first sentence of that quotation is reasonably correct. The
second is only partially correct. The third and fourth are very
largely incorrect. Owens College, Manchester, was founded to
provide instruction in 'such branches of learning and science as
are now and may be hereafter usually taught in the English
Universities'.[1] From the start it taught the classics, English
language and literature, and philosophy, as well as the natural
sciences and mathematics. In fact, many people thought it paid
too much attention to the humanities; within its first ten years it
was accused by the *Manchester Guardian* of 'dissipating itself in
the propagation of a traditional classical curriculum'.[2]

The Nottingham University College combined the work of the
city's Mechanics' Institute with university extension lectures; the
humanities were taught there from the start, along with scientific
and technological subjects. Firth College, Sheffield, was also a
child of the university extension movement; its founder, like
Owens, intended it to be for 'purposes of higher education, and
especially for the teaching and cultivation of any branches of
learning taught or cultivated in the English Universities . . .'[3]
Not until 1897 – nearly twenty years after its foundation – did it
link up with a medical school and a technical college. At Reading
it was the University Extension Association which was the
pioneer; the University College came into being when, in 1892,
the management of the Schools of Science and Art were handed
over to this Association. The Welsh University Colleges were the
result of a long-felt need for 'a University founded on broad and
liberal principles'.[4] Even such an ostensibly scientific establish-

---

[1] See H. B. Charlton, *Portrait of a University*, Manchester
University Press, 1951, p. 26.

[2] Quoted from Charlton, op. cit., pp. 58–9.

[3] See A. W. Chapman, *The Story of a Modern University*, Oxford
University Press, 1955, p. 13.

[4] See D. Emrys Evans, *The University of Wales*, University of
Wales Press, 1953, p. 10.

ment as the Yorkshire College of Science was prepared from the beginning to include the teaching of the arts.

Such a statement as that of Mr Herklots – which has been made on innumerable other occasions – that the modern universities were 'created by industrialism to meet her own needs' is inaccurate in another, and fundamental, respect. The colleges from which the modern universities have sprung were almost all of them brought into being by gifts from private individuals. Among these individuals industrialists undoubtedly figured prominently: not unnaturally, since they were among the wealthiest members of nineteenth century society. But of the three men who gave great sums of money to found colleges only one can be said to have done so with specifically industrial needs in view: Josiah Mason, who altogether gave over £200,000 to the college in Birmingham which for long bore his name. His aim was to 'provide enlarged means of scientific instruction on the scale required by the necessities of the town and district'.[1] Of the others, John Owens' main purpose, for which he bequeathed nearly £100,000, was to found a college, later, he hoped, to become a university, with the educational purposes outlined above, which should also be entirely free from all religious tests, and which was intended for the benefit of the inhabitants of Manchester and South Lancashire.[2] Henry Robinson Hartley, who bequeathed over £100,000 to the Southampton Corporation (alas, over half of this sum was dissipated in law suits over his will), intended that there should be set up in the city, in addition to a public library, a botanical garden and other cultural amenities for the citizens, a college devoted to the 'study and advancement of the sciences of natural history, astronomy, antiquities, and classical and oriental learning'.[3] Mark Firth, too, whose gifts, amounting to some £25,000 in all, launched Firth College at Sheffield, was more interested in general than in vocational education.

But most of the colleges were not created by large individual benefactions. The Yorkshire College of Science, the Newcastle

[1] Quoted from Armytage, op. cit., p. 223. [2] See Charlton, op. cit.
[3] Centenary Commemoration booklet, 1950. Historical note by Professor G. G. Dudley, p. 7.

College of Physical Science, and the Liverpool University College, were launched by public subscription. Welshmen everywhere contributed to the foundation of the Colleges at Aberystwyth, Bangor, and Cardiff. The College of Science at Bristol received financial support from the Merchant Venturers, the local Medical School, the civic authorities, and private donors. Although an anonymous benefactor gave £10,000 towards the foundation of Nottingham University College, this institution came into being mainly through the munificence of the Nottingham Corporation, which voted £100,000 towards the cost of the buildings, and levied a three-halfpenny rate for its maintenance – despite the protests of frugally-minded citizens.

The second point I would emphasise is that, generously though benefactors of colleges contributed – as they often did, whether they were public or corporate bodies, wealthy individuals, or small subscribers – almost none of them realised the scale of financial provision required to establish and maintain a college giving education at a university level. Consequently, most of the colleges quickly found themselves 'in the red', and unable by their own efforts to regain financial solvency. Not surprisingly, they turned to the State for aid; it was the only body left which could give effective assistance.

State grants to British universities were not entirely without precedent; the Scottish universities had received them ever since 1707, and London University from its foundation. But in both cases the circumstances were unusual, and no Government felt itself committed by these precedents to a policy of State aid for university education. Owens College, Manchester, was in 1853 refused a grant on this ground. Nevertheless, in Wales the possibility of State subvention was envisaged from the moment that plans for university colleges in the Principality began to be laid in earnest in 1863. A committee was appointed to set about raising by public subscription the sum of £50,000. Should any further funds be required, it was resolved to call upon Parliament to supply them. It was soon found that additional funds were required. Despite the fact that the committee were fortunate enough to be able to buy in 1867, for the 'knock-down' price of

£10,000, a large hotel at Aberystwyth, when the college opened five years later 'more than three-quarters of the purchase money for the building was still owing.'[1] Appeals for aid were made to the Government, only to receive the reply that it was not the Government's custom to make such grants. So the committee appealed to Welshmen everywhere; and within the following nine years over 100,000 people gave sums of less than half-a-crown towards its support.

But, magnificent though this sustained effort was, it was not enough. In 1879 the college had a balance at the bank of only £319. In a desperate effort to economise, among other measures it dropped its Professor of Music – in Wales of all countries!

Another appeal to the Government was made, this time with success. The success was due to the recommendations of a departmental committee set up in 1880 to inquire into the condition of intermediate (i.e., secondary) and higher education in Wales. The report of this committee, published in 1881, was epoch-making. It resulted in the setting up of a statutory system of secondary education in Wales thirteen years before this happened in England, the foundation of two more university colleges in the Principality, and annual grants of £4,000 from Parliament to each of the Welsh university colleges.

But though the Government gave way in this particular instance, they were not yet prepared to do so on a general scale. They moved cautiously, step by step; or perhaps it would be more accurate to say that they reluctantly gave way step by step to incessant and increasing pressure. In March 1887 they announced that they had decided to grant £2,000 a year to the federal Victoria University of Manchester, founded in 1880 and at the time comprising three Colleges, Owens at Manchester, and the University Colleges of Leeds and Liverpool. This concession naturally gave immense encouragement to all the colleges which were agitating for grants. They renewed their appeals, and at last, in March 1889, the Government, yielding to a pressure which had

---

[1] Emrys Evans, op. cit., p. 18.

by then become clamant as well as persistent, came to the rescue of the poverty-stricken university colleges as a whole. They set down in the Civil Estimates for the year 1889–90 the sum of £15,000 in aid of 'university colleges in Great Britain'; and they appointed a committee of five persons, under the chairmanship of Sir John Lubbock 'to assist in determining the colleges, amongst which, and the proportion in which, the said sum should, if approved by annual Vote of Parliament, be distributed'.[1]

A memorandum, dated March 1st, 1889, presented to the Treasury by the Lord President of the Council and the Chancellor of the Exchequer, defined as follows the kind of recipients expected to share in the grant:

> The class of colleges which it is intended to benefit are the growth of recent years, and have sprung up to meet the demand for higher education in great centres of population among persons who cannot afford to spend two or three years at the old universities. The distinguishing feature of these institutions is that they give teaching of a university standard in arts and science, and are located in populous districts.

Or, to put it very briefly, they were to be recently established, cheap, urban establishments.

The criteria on which the amounts of grant should be determined, the memorandum suggested, should be (i) the quality of the teaching, (ii) the amount of work done, (iii) the income of the institution, (iv) the proportion of income to the average number of students, and (v) the amount of financial support given to the institution from local sources. One of these criteria, the second, calls for particular comment, because a note on it suggested a principle of assessment for aid which, had it become established in its original terms, might have made it considerably more difficult for the colleges to aspire to full university status. The note proposed that the amount of work done in each institution should be tested by (a) the number of students, (b) the average number of lectures attended by each student, and:

[1] Treasury Minute dated March 11th, 1889.

(c) also, perhaps, the amount of additional work that might be fairly demanded in return for the assistance given by the State, especially in the shape of evening lectures accessible to those who, owing to other occupations, are unable to devote the whole of the day to study.

A great deal of such evening work was being done by all the colleges. Almost the whole of it was below university standard, and a great deal of it very much so. Had it been regarded as a *quid pro quo* for State grant the colleges might never have been able to shed it. As it was the task proved long and difficult enough.

Twelve colleges, eleven in England and one in Scotland, hoped to receive a share of the grant. They were:

King's College	London
University College	London
Owens College	Manchester
Mason's College	Birmingham
Firth College	Sheffield
The Yorkshire College	Leeds
University College	Liverpool
University College	Bristol
University College	Nottingham
The Durham College of Science	Newcastle-upon-Tyne
The Hartley Institute	Southampton
University College	Dundee

The total amount of the grant, £15,000, seems pitifully small; and indeed it was far smaller than had been hoped; the colleges had had a figure of something like £50,000 in mind. But, small as it was, it meant in some cases at least all the difference between continuing their work and closing down. The historian of Sheffield University, Dr A. W. Chapman, records[1] that 'the grant almost certainly saved some of the colleges, Firth College among them, from early collapse'. As the total income of Firth College at the time was only £2,200 a year, much of which was guaranteed for

[1] Op. cit., p. 65.

only a few months longer, one can well see why the addition of £1,200 could mean the difference between life and death.

Perhaps the most apt comment on the amount of the total grant was that of Professor W. Ramsay, professor of Chemistry at University College, London, and previously Principal of University College, Bristol, who had been a leader among the appellants. In a letter[1] to the Principal of Firth College, Professor W. M. Hicks, he wrote: 'It is not quite a *ridiculus mus*, but we must regard it as the thin edge of the wedge, and keep on trying to increase it. It will certainly not be withdrawn.'

Ramsay was quite right that the grant would not be withdrawn. Getting it increased was to prove quite another matter.

The 'Committee on Grants to University Colleges in Great Britain', as it was ponderously styled, excluded the Hartley Institute, Southampton, from the list of beneficiaries, on the grounds that it did not possess a professorial staff 'adequate for the complete teaching of university subjects', or, apparently, 'a proper representative governing body'.[2] The committee also suggested that in the future the Dundee University College should be considered along with the Scottish Universities (which had for over half a century been receiving annual Treasury grants); they recommended, however, a grant to it of £500 for the year 1889–90.

Two points made by the Committee in their report upon the criteria by which they had allocated the grant among the colleges deserve particular notice. First, they rejected the idea that 'a certain amount of income from local support' should be required as a qualification for Government grant. They contented themselves with advising that each college should have to submit annually a balance sheet, and should be told that 'in all probability' the Government representatives would, in examining this, pay special attention to 'the amount and character of the local support which is being given to the college'.[3] Secondly, the

[1] Quoted from Chapman, op. cit., p. 62.
[2] *Report of the Committee on Grants to University Colleges in Great Britain*, undated, but presented between March 11th and July 1st, 1889.   [3] Ibid., p. 5.

Committee thought it 'desirable that a person representing the Government should visit each college from time to time'. But – and the point was to prove crucially important – such visitation was:

> not for the purpose of examining the students, but to inspect buildings and laboratories, and to become personally acquainted with the nature and extent of the different courses of study.[1]

The Lords of the Treasury did not in 1889 apparently contemplate any future alteration in the total amount of the grant, but they recognised that the 'relative claims of the several colleges' would vary from time to time, and so they proposed that (provided Parliament continued the grant) its allocation should be reviewed every five years.

The first 'quinquennium' was, however, to prove a long one. Although the Grants Committee recommended in 1892, and again in 1894, that the total grant should be increased to £30,000, no increase was sanctioned until 1897, except that in 1892–3 £500 a year was added for a new member, the Bedford College for Women, London.

In 1897–8 the total grant was increased to £25,000, and there it remained until 1903–4, when £2,000 was added to provide for Reading and Southampton, which were then included in the grant list.

In 1904, however, there was a dramatic development. In February the Chancellor of the Exchequer promised a deputation from the colleges[2] that he would ask Parliament to double the grant, to £54,000, in 1904–5, and said that he hoped it might be increased to £100,000 in 1905–6. A new committee was set up, and invited to report 'how, in their opinion, State-aid to University teaching can be most effectively organised and applied'. This committee, the Chancellor thought, 'need not be bound by the

[1] Ibid., pp. 5–6.

[2] Treasury Minute dated March 30th, 1904. It is interesting to note that although by this time four of the 'Colleges' were full Universities, the Minute makes no reference to the fact.

principles laid down for the guidance of former committees', but 'should pay special regard to the following points':

(1) Assistance should be given to those institutions only which afford education of a University standard in great centres of population.

(2) Assistance should be given with the object of stimulating private benevolence in the locality.

(3) The present requirements of a minimum local income of £4,000 and of £1,500 from fees should be maintained.

The first of these requirements faced the new universities and the university colleges with the formidable task of making clear what parts of their work were 'of a university standard'. That they tackled this task energetically and successfully seems clear from the fact that the two Inspectors who paid visits to all the colleges were able to report in 1907[1] that 'since the universities have extended their aegis over various technological subjects it no longer rests with us to give a definition of "subjects of university rank".' But while the distinction between 'degree' and 'non-degree' work had become reasonably clear, most of the universities and colleges were still carrying a huge load of the latter. At Sheffield, for instance, in 1907–8, of a total of 2,170 students (734 day and 1,436 evening) only 139 were doing degree courses and three post-graduate work. This case was typical.

The doctrine that the function of State-aid to universities was to stimulate private benevolence was reiterated in practically every report of the University Colleges Committee and of its successor, the University Grants Committee (set up in 1919), right down to 1939. Perhaps the most extreme statement is that in the Board of Education's report for 1908–9 on Universities and University Colleges in receipt of Treasury Grant:[2]

State-aid to university teaching would, however, be of doubtful advantage if it did not stimulate private effort and induce bene-

[1] Appendix to the University Colleges Committee's report dated June 6th, 1907: p. 13.

[2] H.M.S.O., 1910, p. iv.

factors to contribute in the present day as they did in the olden times, to give of their wealth for the support of that higher learning upon which now, more than ever 'the prosperity, even the very safety and existence, of our country depend'.

But twenty-five years later, in their last quinquennial report before the second world war,[1] the U.G.C. were insisting that 'the call for continued and indeed for increased assistance from all and every outside source is greater than ever', because 'a university's general endowment fund is the surest foundation upon which to build its independence and stability'.

But though the universities and colleges received many notable gifts, benefactors did not, in fact, contribute 'as they did in the olden times'. The inevitable result of the proportionate decline in this source of revenue, coupled with the State's frugal-minded reliance upon the principle of self-help, was that throughout the whole period from 1889 to 1939 the modern universities and university colleges were rarely able to rise above the level of bare subsistence. This was frequently acknowledged in the Grants Committees' reports. 'We have seen no single College in which adequate funds were available for departmental expenditure', wrote their inspectors in 1901.[2] In 1913 a memorandum (undated and unsigned, but written after 1909) from a deputation which urged the Chancellor of the Exchequer to 'assist in providing adequate sums' for university development stated that 'for the most part the Universities and University Colleges have developed to the utmost point that is possible with the income at present at their disposal'. And in their *Returns from Universities and University Colleges in Receipt of Treasury Grant*, for the year 1920–1, the recently established University Grants Committee recorded[3] that:

. . . of the 45 Universities and Colleges which carry forward a balance on revenue account, 29 incurred deficits on the year's

[1] University Grants Committee, *Report for the period 1929–30 to 1934–5*, H.M.S.O., 1936, p. 10.

[2] Report by Dr H. G. Woods and Dr A. Hill, dated December 31st, 1901, p. 7.   [3] Section 9.

working – some of these deficits are very considerable . . .
moreover, 25 Institutions show accumulated deficits as at
July 31st, 1921; in some cases these amounts are very large.
Twenty Institutions are the fortunate possessors of accumulated
surpluses, but with one or two exceptions these are of moderate
amount. There are instances in which the Balance Sheets reveal
large debts on capital account.

All that the U.G.C. was able to offer to the starving institutions
– swollen at the time by many thousands of ex-service students –
was the bleak advice that:

It is evident that the financial situation of the Institutions continues to demand rigorous economy, and the concentration of
effort upon consolidating existing activities.

Such advice was the more likely because the universities and
colleges were by then largely dependent upon their Treasury
grants. These had been increased fivefold in the ten years preceding the first world war, from the £54,000 of 1904–5 to
£275,147. Immediately after the war they were more than
doubled. In 1920–1 the total came to £593,708. But the number of
students had also more than doubled: in England from 12,038 in
1913–14 to 24,963 in 1920–1; and the value of money had
seriously diminished. Moreover, a factor not susceptible to exact
measurement, the proportion of full-time students to the total
number had been greatly enlarged.

If ever centres of higher learning came up the hard way, the
modern English universities did. Though their financial position
improved during the inter-war years, largely owing to increased
Treasury grants, which by 1939 amounted to 36·2 per cent of
their total income, even in that year eight out of fifty-nine still
had a debit balance – and all the rest could have spent many times
their income on essential developments.

CHAPTER FIVE

The making of a University calls for inspiration and for enterprise. –
H.R.H. THE PRINCESS ROYAL.[1]

Financial difficulties were by no means the only troubles which
afflicted the Colleges during their apprenticeship – though lack of
money was at the root of most of them. Owens College nearly died
in its early days for lack of students, and Aberystwyth languished
for nearly a decade for the same reason. These were somewhat
unusual experiences; what was far more common was that, as the
historians of Bristol University put it, 'there were always twice as
many evening students, who were really the life-blood of the little
college, and there was every danger that the "undergraduates"
proper would have no feeling of cohesion'.[2]

Very frequently colleges were handicapped by having to begin
in inadequate or unsuitable buildings. Bristol opened in a terrace
house, Liverpool in a disused lunatic asylum (as also did Leicester
nearly forty years later). At Reading a start was made in a school
of art and a school of science rented to the college by the town
council; to these were added shortly afterwards a vicarage. At
Sheffield the building which had been designed and erected for
Firth College was within a dozen years so overcrowded that much
practical work in physics was being done in the College hall,
which also housed the library, and on landings, while 'the staff
had no common room, and even the Principal had no private

[1] In the Foreword to *The University of Leeds, The First Half-
Century*, by A. N. Shimmin. Cambridge University Press, 1954.
p. xi.

[2] *The Life of a University*, by Basil Cottle and J. W. Sherborne.
Published for the University of Bristol by J. W. Arrowsmith Ltd.,
1951, p. 10.

room of his own'.[1] In 1901 the Grants Committee's inspectors noted[2] that 'in almost all the Colleges' there was a 'want of suitable common rooms, reading rooms and refectories for students'. Problems of accommodation were perpetually to harass the Colleges, and did not cease when they became Universities; indeed, they are with them still.

Recruitment of teachers was another perennial problem. Salaries were low, and, as has been shown, facilities for teaching meagre. Lack of funds usually precluded the appointment of a sufficiently large teaching staff, with the result that teachers were frequently heavily over-worked. This overwork was accentuated by the fact that the students, and public opinion, incessantly demanded results, in the form of examination successes. If these were not produced, the students went elsewhere. As the Government inspectors already quoted said:[3]

> Technical and Municipal schools are competing for students with the Colleges, and a slight falling-off in the efficiency of a College as a place which prepares students for certificates, diplomas, and degrees would result in a serious diminution in the numbers of its students.

In such circumstances, the inspectors commented, 'the teachers have no alternative but to reduce to a pulp the mental nutriment with which they feed their pupils'. And they came to the terrible conclusion[4] that:

> If consulted by a young Oxford or Cambridge graduate of first-class ability as to the course he should pursue, we should, in the light of our experience, advise him to make a great sacrifice to remain at his University rather than to run the risk of muffling his intellect in the multiplied classes of elementary students and the anxious administrative work in which he will find himself enveloped at a Provincial College.

[1] Chapman, op. cit., p. 87.
[2] *University Colleges* (*Great Britain*) (*Grant in Aid*). Report by Dr H. G. Woods and Dr Alex Hill. H.M.S.O., 1902, p. 7.
[3] Loc. cit., p. 10.   [4] Ibid.

The full force of this advice can only be realised when it is recalled that, following extensive reforms forced upon Oxford and Cambridge by Royal Commissions in the 1850s, these universities had marched forward to what was probably their 'finest hour' since their foundation. I think there can be little doubt that between about 1870 and 1914 Oxford and Cambridge rose to greater heights, both intellectually and socially, than ever before.

Happily for the 'Provincial Colleges' there was during these years, as there has been since, a constant (though never large enough) stream of courageous men and women prepared to accept the risk of serving in them. Under the inspiring leadership of men such as Alfred Marshall at Bristol, Arthur Smithells at Leeds, H. E. Roscoe and A. W. Ward at Manchester, W. M. Childs at Reading, W. M. Hicks at Sheffield, and Viriamu Jones at Cardiff – the list could be continued almost indefinitely – the Colleges gradually reduced their disabilities and improved their academic standing. In the latter endeavour they were greatly assisted by the strange chance that had given the University of London the power to grant 'external' degrees, for they proved their right to the title of University largely by preparing successfully their students for its examinations.

The first University charter was gained in 1880 by Manchester. It was not exactly what Manchester had wanted, for the Privy Council refused to give Owens College a charter all to itself, but created instead the Victoria University of Manchester, a federal institution, with Owens College as a constituent member. In 1884 the Liverpool University College, and in 1887 the Yorkshire College at Leeds, also became constituent members. The federation was never altogether happy, and it did not last very long; but at any rate it was a start, and it raised hopes in other places.

The next successful applicant, in 1893, was Wales. In this country geography virtually imposed a federal constitution, because, as Principal Viriamu Jones, its leading advocate, said, 'The various Colleges of Wales will be isolated units until the University of Wales exists, not in name, but in fact.'[1] In 1898

[1] K. Viriamu Jones, *Life of John Viriamu Jones:* quoted by D. Emrys Evans in *The University of Wales, A Historical Sketch,* University of Wales Press, 1953, p. 36.

Joseph Chamberlain, then approaching the peak of his political fame, was made first president of Mason University College, and immediately set to work to make this the University of Birmingham. Within two years he had succeeded. Birmingham's elevation immediately prompted aspirations at Liverpool. With Manchester's agreement the federal Victoria University was dissolved, and Manchester (1903), Liverpool (1903) and Leeds (1904) received separate charters. Sheffield, which had been rejected (very rudely) when it applied for membership of the Victoria University, now tried on its own, and was granted a charter in 1905. Finally, in 1909 Bristol also was made a university. Thus within ten years England more than doubled the number of its universities.

Several circumstances assisted the new universities in their early years: the establishment in 1902 of a statutory system of secondary education; an increasingly favourable and understanding public opinion; an outburst of generosity from private benefactors, who between 1902 and 1907 donated some £1,200,000; increased grants from local education authorities; very substantially increased Treasury grants; and, not least important, recognition by the Treasury[1] of the principle that:

> If State aid to Universities and University Colleges is to be fully effective, a degree of freedom must be allowed in the working of these institutions which is not possible, and indeed is not desirable, in the case of schools.

In this favourable climate the new universities, and the university colleges, made substantial and gratifying progress. As early as 1907 the Government inspectors were able to report[2] that:

> There is a University spirit incapable of definition which pervades the several University Colleges in a greater or less degree,

[1] See Report of Advisory Committee dated July 24th, 1908, p. 2, and Treasury Minute on the Committee's Report dated June 3rd, 1909, p. 8. H.M.S.O., 1909.
[2] Report to the University Colleges Committee by Sir Thomas Raleigh and Dr Alex Hill. Appendix to Report of the Committee dated June 6th, 1907, p. 11.

influencing the intellectual growth of their students and producing, as we think, results of the highest importance which
are not capable of expression in tables of examination successes.

The inspectors went on to testify to the 'zeal and devotion' of
the teaching staffs, saying that it was the more admirable in view
of the fact that 'the large majority of the students never get beyond
the more elementary stages'; and teachers therefore rarely had
'opportunity of giving advanced instruction or of discussing problems which from their difficulty may still be said to have an
interest for themselves'. This problem of the student unfitted by
ability or attainments to undertake work of university standard
was the most stubborn educational problem with which the universities and colleges had to cope; but good progress towards
mastering it had been made before 1914.

The new universities had hardly got into their stride before the
first world war broke out. It dealt them, as it did the older
universities, a fearful blow. Recruitment to the armed forces was
in 1914 and part of 1915 completely voluntary, and based on an
appeal to patriotism and self-respect. 'Your King and Country
need you.' The cream of British youth responded almost to a
man – and were swept indiscriminately into the front line, many
thousands of them to perish in the holocaust of the Somme and
subsequent organised slaughters. The universities and colleges
were bereft between 1914 and 1919 of most of their ablest
students and younger teaching staff – and have suffered right
down to the present day from the lack of those who did not return.

After the war demobilisation and re-entry into civilian life were
almost as uncontrolled as had been recruitment to the Forces in
1914. The Government were generous to the men and women
who wished to resume or undertake university studies. Grants to
them were made available on the easiest terms, with the result that
within twelve months after the cease-fire every university institution in the United Kingdom was crammed to bursting point. In
the academic year 1913–14 there had been 22,234 full-time
university students; in 1919–20 there were already 36,424, and in
1920–1 there were 40,130.

In the light of the ideas prevalent at the time, the Government were also generous in providing funds for the universities. The recurrent Treasury grant was within the two years 1919–21 increased to double the 1913–14 figure, and during the same period grants amounting to about £700,000 were made for capital expenditure – despite the fact that since 1908, if not earlier, the principle had been firmly established that 'the main object of the Treasury grants is maintenance rather than initial or capital expenditure'.[1]

Though the total number of students declined somewhat as the ex-service students passed out, and again during the second half of the 1930s, it never fell substantially. Throughout the inter-war years it remained at rather more than double the 1913–14 figure. Nor did the Treasury grants for recurrent expenditure decrease; on the contrary, they were steadily increased, rising from about £790,000 in 1919–20 to just over £2,000,000 in 1938–9, by which time they constituted some 36 per cent of the universities' and colleges' income.[2] Even the world-wide economic crisis of 1928–31 was not allowed to check the flow. But as these grants were made throughout the period on the same basis as previously, that is, as a supplement to income and a spur to local generosity, and as grants for capital expenditure were rare after the first few years, the universities and colleges were in general unable to do nearly as much in the way of development as they would have liked. Many, indeed, were hard put to it to maintain all their existing activities in good heart. A few were fortunate. Private benefactions enabled Birmingham to erect fine new buildings on its Edgbaston property, Leeds, Nottingham, and the University College of the South-West at Exeter to move on to more spacious sites, and Reading, which received a university charter in 1926, to realise in large part its ambition to become a fully residential university. London, after having courageously refused in 1920 an offer from the Government of 11½ acres of land in Bloomsbury because of

[1] See Report of Advisory Committee dated July 24th, 1908, p. 4, H.M.S.O., 1909.

[2] This is including Oxford and Cambridge, which received grants from 1926 onwards.

the conditions attached – the sale of the King's College site – was enabled seven years later, thanks to the Rockefeller Trust, to buy the same land and erect thereon a suitably impressive head-quarters for a metropolitan university.

All the universities and colleges benefited both numerically and financially from a practice – after the second world war to be abandoned as pernicious – which was begun by the Board of Education in 1911. This was to offer to prospective teachers grants-in-aid for a four-year university course – three years to take a degree and one year for professional training – in return for a pledge to teach in schools maintained by local education authori-ties. The offer was particularly attractive during the years of heavy industrial unemployment; and numerous parents seized upon it as the one sure means of preventing their children from suffering the anxieties and hardships they themselves were enduring. Teaching, they realised, was a secure and pensionable occupation. Conse-quently, the secondary schools were flooded with able children who knew at the age of eleven what their adult career would be, provided only they passed the requisite examinations, and the universities with students who entered, not primarily because of any love of learning (though many later acquired this), but because that was the way to a safe and certain job for life. And so it was until the latter part of the 1930s, when over-production brought unemployment into the teaching profession. The schools got a lot of good teachers, and the universities – well, Professor Armytage has put it in words I cannot better:[1]

> Indeed it is not too much to say that the civic universities in their struggling years, and the university colleges all along, owed the very existence of their arts faculties and in many cases their pure science faculties to the presence of a large body of intend-ing teachers whose attendance at degree courses was almost guaranteed by the state.

These twenty years were in truth years of struggle for the modern universities and colleges. On the whole, of highly suc-cessful struggle. None collapsed; not even the two newcomers who

[1] Op. cit., p. 256.

joined their ranks, the University Colleges of Leicester (1918) and Hull (1927), even though these went unrecognised and without State aid throughout the whole period. All consolidated their positions; they established new Faculties and Departments, chiefly but not exclusively in scientific and technological disciplines; they attracted to themselves a greater number of distinguished teachers and more able and better prepared students; they rid themselves of most of their prematriculation work, and increased their post-graduate studies and research; they built new libraries, laboratories, lecture rooms, and halls of residence, and acquired larger playing fields – though often at an uncomfortable distance from the university buildings.

It would not be correct to say that they came to their full strength during this period; they were too under-nourished for that. But they came as near to it as was possible in the circumstances, and so were able, when the call came to them to face a gigantic expansion, as it did during the second world war, to respond to it with confidence.

PART II

Present

CHAPTER ONE

Two things are required: a considerable expansion of university teaching and research, and more positive planning in the field of university work. —SIR ERNEST SIMON ([later] LORD SIMON OF WYTHENSHAWE).[1]

'The present' is an elastic term. Here it is stretched to cover a period of nearly twenty years, from the early part of the second world war, when plans for post-war expansion of university education in Great Britain first began to be discussed, to the time of writing this book, that is, the year 1960.

These years have seen the opening phases – in view of what is already projected for the near future, and what may well happen later, it would be imprudent to use any more final description than that – of an expansion and development of university and other higher education in Great Britain which, in respect of both size and character, is without precedent in the history of our country. Before attempting an analysis of this expansion (so far as it has gone), and an examination of some of the manifold problems which it has created or exacerbated, it is necessary to consider the war-time planning which enabled it to be set in motion swiftly and, by comparison with 1919, smoothly, after the cessation of hostilities.

Few among our national characteristics make one feel more proud of being British than the superb self-confidence which enables us to sit down, quietly, at times of direst national peril, in order to plan a better order of society for the days when the danger shall have passed – as we invariably assume implicitly it will. Such self-confidence was never more notably displayed than during the second world war, for it was in the black days of 1941

[1] *The Development of British Universities*, Longmans, 1944, p. 3.

and 1942, when to the impartial observer it seemed highly doubtful whether there would be any future at all for Britain – at least
as a free and independent country – that the British began to plan
in earnest social reform on the largest scale. And, as they had done
in previous wars, they began with educational reform – an inter-
estingly curious choice for a people commonly regarded (even by
itself) to be apathetic in its attitude to public education.

I have not been able to discover who first began to advocate
university expansion (not that it matters), but the British Association for the Advancement of Science was certainly early in the
field. In September 1941 its Division for the Social and International Relations of Science held a Conference on Science and
World Order; at this the questions of university education after
the war and the rehabilitation of universities destroyed or damaged
during the war figured prominently. The upshot of the delibera-
tions of this conference was that the Association appointed a
Committee, under the chairmanship of the late Dr J. C. Maxwell
Garnett, to consider and report upon these matters. This Com-
mittee produced an Interim Report in September 1942, and in
July 1943 a series of Reports:[1] on University Finance in Great
Britain, University Entrance Scholarships in England and Wales,
Education for the Public Service, and Universities and Adult
Education. Along with these Reports were published also two
'Notes': one on 'Universities and the Education of Teachers', and
one setting out a scheme for a Universities Advisory Council
whose function should be 'to consider the whole range of univer-
sity policy' and 'to effect co-ordination and eliminate any unnecessary or wasteful overlapping'.

Among the numerous recommendations made by the Committee
there was one, in their Report on university finance, which – as
they realised – went to the heart of the matter. '*The Treasury Grant
should be at once doubled after the war.*' The actual amount proposed, some £4,800,000 in place of £2,400,000, was not the
significant feature of this recommendation: indeed, by comparison
with the recommendation made almost simultaneously by the

[1] The Reports were published one by one during September and
October, 1943.

Parliamentary and Scientific Committee[1] that the grant be raised to £6,000,000 or £7,000,000, it was quite modest. The significance of the recommendation lay in the argument supporting it. Hitherto, said the Committee:

> . . . in the main, State and local assistance . . . has been for the most part an addition to income and has not been available to any large extent for capital expenditure.
>
> *It is, in our view, to this source that the universities must look in the immediate future for their major development.*[2]

This implied a complete reversal of the financial policy hitherto consistently maintained by every Government.

That the Committee were fully aware of the significance of this recommendation is shown by their comment, made later in the Report, that 'the crux of the whole matter lies in this change in the incidence of university income which is fundamental . . .'

When they made this recommendation the British Association Committee were thinking in terms of an immediate increase of 50 per cent over the 1938-9 numbers of students in the universities of Great Britain. The Association of University Teachers, which had also been discussing post-war expansion from an early date, published early in 1944 a report advocating the same proportionate increase. This appears to have been at the time a fairly widely accepted estimate, though some members of the A.U.T. thought it conservative, and the editor of the Association's journal doubted whether it 'would prove sufficient in the long run'. A demand by the National Union of Students that the university population be increased by 300 to 400 per cent within the next ten to twenty years seemed to most people in 1944 to be wildly unrealistic, but the numbers achieved by 1960 and those projected for 1970 suggest that the N.U.S. were not quite so starry-eyed as their critics imagined. The Parliamentary and Scientific Committee, looking (like the N.U.S.) farther ahead than the first few years, were not quite so ambitious: the universities, they thought, as the

[1] In a Report on *Scientific Research and the Universities in Post-War Britain*, published by the Committee in October 1943.

[2] p. 3.

only institutions capable of training creative research workers, would 'need to handle ultimately something like two to three times the 1938–9 number of science and technology students', and, since there could be 'no question of reducing the numbers in other subjects in order to get more scientists', might have possibly to look to 'an ultimate doubling of the total numbers enjoying university education'. The much larger increase in the Treasury grant proposed by this Committee was the inevitable consequence of their forecast of student numbers.

The Parliamentary and Scientific Committee forecast fairly accurately not only the numerical expansion which has since taken place, but also the way in which it has been distributed among the English universities:

> As those of our universities which now have 5,000 or 6,000 students are probably near the maximum desirable size, this implies a great expansion of the remaining establishments and possibly the development and promotion of some existing establishments, such as the university colleges, to university rank, or even the foundation of new universities.

These early generalised explorations were followed during the next three years by a veritable spate of reports by governmental committees which specified the particular increases they felt necessary in their fields. Here is the list:

1944

Report of the Inter-Departmental Committee on Medical Schools (The 'Goodenough' Report).
Committee on Veterinary Education in Great Britain. Second Report.
Teachers and Youth Leaders (The 'McNair' Report).
Teachers: Supply, Recruitment and Training in the Period immediately following the war. Report of the Advisory Council on Education in Scotland.

1945

Higher Technological Education (The 'Percy' Report).

Final Report of the Inter-Departmental Committee on Dentistry (The 'Teviot' Report).
Committee on Agricultural Education in Scotland (The 'Alness' Report).

1946

Scientific Man-Power (The 'Barlow' Report).
Report of the Committee on the study of Oriental, Slavonic, East European and African languages (The 'Scarbrough' Report).
Report of the Committee on Higher Agricultural Education in England and Wales (The 'Loveday' Report).
Report of the Committee on the Provision for Social and Economic Research (The 'Clapham' Report).

Every one of these reports demanded from the universities a larger annual intake of students in their specialties. In some cases the proportional increases demanded were substantial; dentistry, for example, wanted 800 students a year in place of 340, education 4,400 in place of 2,800. Other similar demands were made in non-governmental reports published during these years or shortly after, such as the report of a Special Committee set up by the Royal Institute of British Architects on Architectural Education, published in 1946, and a report by Miss Eileen Younghusband undertaken for the Carnegie United Kingdom Trust, and published in 1947, on the Employment and Training of Social Workers. This last made proportionately the largest demand of all; it asked that the annual intake of students who would prepare for careers in social work be stepped up from 250 to 875. During the same period estimates of their future needs for highly qualified recruits were made by the Civil Service Commission and the Colonial Office, and by the Churches and other professions seeking university graduates. Altogether, it has been estimated,[1] the demands from these various sources called for an annual output

[1] See *The Problem Facing British Universities*. Nuffield College Report: Oxford University Press, 1948, Table I, p. 12, and pp. 11–28.

of some 22,000 qualified men and women, in place of the pre-war output of 14,000. Only law and the churches were satisfied with the totals of their previous intakes.

Among the governmental reports one was outstanding. Because of the size and the general nature of its demands – for 'scientists and technologists' – the Barlow Report on *Scientific Man-Power* made by far the greatest impact on public opinion. This document is, indeed, of considerable historical importance; more than any of the others it determined both the character and the numerical dimension of post-war university expansion. It is, therefore, examined here in some detail.

The 'Barlow' Committee (Chairman, Sir Alan Barlow) was appointed by the Lord President of the Council in December 1945:

> to consider the policies which should govern the use and development of our scientific man-power and resources during the next ten years and to submit a report on very broad lines at an early date so as to facilitate forward planning in those fields which are dependent upon the use of scientific man-power.

The committee worked at speed. They presented their Report in April 1946; and it was published in May. The Committee came to the conclusion that in 1945–6 it was unlikely that Great Britain had at its disposal more than 55,000 qualified scientists, that is, 'persons holding degrees in the mathematical, physical, chemical and biological sciences', together with a few non-graduates who were 'members of recognised scientific institutions with a membership status that is accepted as the equivalent of a university degree in these subjects'. They estimated that the minimum demand for scientific workers thus qualified would by 1950 be 70,000; and they added that this figure was probably an underestimate, and possibly a serious one. They then went on to say that:

> It is only to the Universities that we can look for any substantial recruitment to the ranks of qualified scientists. The proportion

that has come from other sources in the past is very small indeed and we do not favour any attempt to add a responsibility for producing a substantial number of pure scientists to the existing and prospective burdens of the Technical Colleges. Generally speaking, the university is an essential stage in a scientist's education and in any event the Technical Colleges will be hard put to it to produce the number of technologists that are required to support and apply the work of the scientists.

The Committee, it will be seen, drew a clear distinction between the educational functions of the university and the technical college. Some people were inclined to query the validity of the distinction; in view of this it is interesting to note that the membership of the committee did not include anyone who could be called representative of the technical colleges.

Before the war, the Committee stated, the British universities were producing about 2,500 scientists a year. In response to an enquiry put to them in May 1945 they had estimated that in the aggregate they could within a decade increase the numbers of their students by about 45 per cent over the pre-war strength.[1] This meant, the Committee calculated, an output rising to 3,500 a year by 1955. Allowing for wastage, an annual output of this order could not be expected to produce by that year a total force of more than 64,000 qualified scientists. But by then the country would need at least 90,000. In short, the universities' offer, munificent though at first sight it appeared to be, was not nearly large enough. 'We are satisfied', said the Committee, that 'the immediate aim should be to double the present output, giving us roughly 5,000 newly qualified scientists per annum at the earliest possible moment.' This increase was not to be achieved at the expense of students of other subjects, and the Committee would deprecate any attempt to do so.

Was such an increase practicable? The Committee had no doubt that it was:

[1] Oxford and Cambridge thought they could not expand at all; the English civic universities thought they might expand some 85 per cent.

At present rather less than two per cent of the population reach the universities. About five per cent of the whole population show, on test, an intelligence as great as the upper half of the students, who amount to one per cent of the population. We conclude, therefore, that only about one in five of the boys and girls, who have intelligence equal to that of the best half of the university students, actually reach the universities.

Allowing for the fact that some of those who did not reach the university might not possess 'the other innate capacities necessary to a university career,' and that others 'would not desire a university career,' it still seemed clear to the Committee that there was 'an ample reserve of intelligence in the country to allow both a doubling of the university numbers and at the same time a raising of standards'.

The Committee's estimate of the proportion of potential university students in the total population was based partly on the national distribution of intelligence as measured by standardised tests, and partly on sample testings of graduates, made at Scottish universities by the late Professor Sir Godfrey Thomson, and of undergraduates at Manchester University by Dr Leybourne-White. It was widely criticised at the time, and has since been recurrently criticised, as over-optimistic, but, so far as I know, no researches by investigators of comparable standing have proved it wrong.

The Committee recognised the manifold obstacles in the way of providing quickly the staff and accommodation necessary to provide for anything approaching so large a number of students. But, first, money had to be available. Where was it to come from? The Committee were in no doubt:

> The great bulk of the money required for university development must come from the Exchequer and we are satisfied that more than any other single factor, the universities' response to any call for expansion will depend upon a wise and generous financial policy towards them on the part of the Government.

The Committee did not specify any sum as desirable; they contented themselves with saying that they were glad to note that the

Treasury grant for 1946–7 had been increased from £5·65 millions to £9·45 millions, and that the Chancellor of the Exchequer had told the University Grants Committee that he would consider asking Parliament to vote even larger amounts; and with expressing the hope that it would be possible for the Government 'to persuade the universities that in future they will be able to rely upon adequate and continuing assistance from the Exchequer towards any project for which . . . good cause is shown'.

Though the Barlow Report had an outstanding effect, every one of the reports that I have listed affected the size and pattern of post-war university education. Some did so importantly; notable among these was the report of the Goodenough Committee, which effected something like a revolution in medical education. The report of the Percy Committee, which covered a wider field than university education, achieved the unenviable distinction of touching off (or perhaps one should say reviving) a controversy between the universities and the technical colleges which was to rage for ten years, and indeed, if some present-day expressions of opinion are to be relied upon, has not yet been entirely resolved.

In brief, this controversy revolved around the question of whether the technical colleges, or some such institution as a 'Royal College of Technologists' which would have authority on their behalf, should or should not have the right to award degrees. The technical colleges put up a strong and persistent battle for the honour, but the universities were inflexibly opposed to it, and in the end gained the day. There were many subsidiary issues involved, but essentially the dispute was concerned with status and prestige.

The Percy Committee was appointed by the Minister of Education in April 1944:

> to consider the needs of higher technological education in England and Wales and the respective contribution to be made thereto by Universities and Technical Colleges.

One of the Committee's main general conclusions was that:

> Industry must look mainly to Universities for the training of scientists, both for research and development, and of teachers

of science; it must look mainly to Technical Colleges for technical assistants and craftsmen. But both Universities and Colleges must share the responsibility for educating the future senior administrators and technically qualified managers of industry.

On the other hand, the Percy Committee felt that 'neither university nor technical college courses are designed of themselves alone to produce a trained engineer'. The Committee accordingly proposed that there should be provided, for about one-third of the annual output of trained engineers, a course equal in length to a university degree course and made up of alternate periods of full-time study and works practice, and for a rather smaller proportion of specially planned courses, different from but 'of a standard comparable with, that of University degree courses'.

Eleven years were to elapse before the 'Diploma in Technology' (Dip. Tech.), an award for technical college students comparable in standard with a university honours degree, was created, and the 'sandwich' courses in which students could prepare for it became a considerable feature in English higher education.

One other Report must be referred to, the McNair Report on *Teachers and Youth Leaders*, because this added a new branch to the university tree. A recommendation – made, incidentally, by only one half of the Committee – that the universities of England and Wales (the Committee was not concerned with Scotland) should accept responsibility for the academic aspects of the training of teachers, was accepted by the universities. To carry out this responsibility they set up Institutes (in two cases called 'Schools') of Education, to supervise and co-ordinate the training of teachers, and to promote the further study of education, within geographical areas attached to the universities. Three universities, Cambridge, Liverpool, and Reading, at first declined to accept this responsibility, but later Liverpool and Reading changed their minds. At the time of writing, Cambridge alone stands outside the scheme.

CHAPTER TWO

The great bulk of the money required for university development must come from the Exchequer . . .[1]

The Universities entirely accept the view that the Government has not only the right but the duty to satisfy itself that every field of study which in the national interest ought to be cultivated in Great Britain is in fact being adequately cultivated in the University system, and that the resources which are placed at the disposal of the Universities are being used with full regard both to efficiency and to economy.[2]

While this great volume of report-making was going on the universities, in conjunction with the University Grants Committee, had been conducting their own investigations into the possibilities of expansion after the war. In June 1943 the Committee of Vice-Chancellors and Principals, which throughout the war acted as the spokesman of the universities with the Government, asked the U.G.C. to 'set on foot a review of the financial implications of the expansion which national policy would require the universities to undertake, both in the immediate future and in the next ten or twenty years'.[3] They asked that special reference might be given to:

>   (i) the capital and maintenance costs of new lands and build-
>   ings;

[1] *Scientific Man-power:* Report of a Committee appointed by the Lord President of the Council. Cmd. 6824. H.M.S.O., 1946, p. 11.

[2] Committee of Vice-Chancellors and Principals. *A Note on University Policy and Finance in the Decennium 1947–56.* Privately printed, 1946, p. 14.

[3] Quoted from *University Development from 1935 to 1947.* Report of the University Grants Committee. H.M.S.O., 1948, p. 76.

(ii) the cost of maintaining adequate teaching establishments adequately paid;

(iii) the cost of maintaining and developing fundamental research.

It is clear that even at this early date the Committee of Vice-Chancellors and Principals had realised that in the future – and the immediate future at that – the universities would have a moral obligation to undertake specific tasks in the interests of national policy. Equally, the Committee had also realised that this would imply on the part of the universities a financial dependence on the Government in respect of both recurrent and capital expenditure. They pointed out, first, that private benefactions to the universities for capital expenditure would diminish after the war, and that therefore expansion 'would necessitate non-recurrent grants from the Exchequer on a scale not hitherto contemplated', and secondly, that, as it was unlikely that the universities' 'revenue from non-governmental sources could be greatly increased', 'a major part of the new expenditure to be incurred by the universities would have to be financed by the Exchequer'.[1]

In November 1943 the U.G.C. replied to the Committee's request by asking the universities and university colleges to draw up proposals, including estimated capital and recurrent costs, for development over the following ten years. Such proposals were duly forwarded to the U.G.C. early in 1944. In January 1945 the U.G.C., after having had discussions with representatives of all the universities and colleges, presented to the Treasury a memorandum showing the estimated financial requirements for this period as agreed between themselves and the universities and colleges. In this memorandum the U.G.C.

emphasised the argument that the universities had reached a critical point in their history and that the expansion and improvement of facilities for university education which the public interest demanded could be achieved only with the aid of largely increased subventions from the Exchequer.[2]

[1] Ibid.   [2] Ibid.

The Treasury accepted the argument, and in April 1945 the Chancellor of the Exchequer announced that, in accordance with recommendations made by the U.G.C., the annual grant to the universities and university colleges would, during the first two years after the war, be increased from £2,149,000 (the figure at which it had been stabilised during the war) to £4,149,000. The Chancellor also, again on the recommendation of the U.G.C., gave the universities and colleges an assurance that the grant would be substantially increased during the other years of the decade for which their estimates had been made.

The promise given was fulfilled. The principle of assessing grants to the universities and colleges on a quinquennial basis was resumed in 1947, and the Chancellor of the Exchequer then announced that the annual grants to the universities for recurrent expenditure during the quinquennium 1947–52 would be as follows:[1]

1947–8	£8,850,000
1948–9	£10,317,775
1949–50	£13,635,470
1950–1	£15,222,408
1951–2	£16,600,113

Part of the value of the large increase in the grants must be discounted because of the rapid fall in the value of money during these years. Even allowing for this, however, the net increase was substantial – though far from being as great as the universities could have wished. Constitutionally, the significant fact was that by 1951–2 the proportion of the universities' and colleges' total income derived from recurrent Treasury grants was more than double what it had been in 1938–9. It had risen from 31·4 per cent to 64·5 per cent.[2]

The Government were prepared to be equally, if not more, generous about grants for capital expenditure: but unhappily good intentions were frustrated by shortages of manpower and

[1] Figures from *University Development: Report on the Years* 1947 *to* 1952. H.M. Stationery Office, 1953. Appendix III, p. 82.

[2] Ibid., p. 11.

materials for building. The U.G.C. told the Chancellor of the Exchequer in January 1947 that they estimated the capital needs of the universities for the quinquennium 1947–52 at about £40,000,000 for new building and £10,000,000 for sites and equipment; and indicated that most of this would have to come from the Exchequer, if it were to be forthcoming at all. The Chancellor promptly accepted the programme in principle; but he felt compelled to warn the U.G.C. that, in his opinion, with the existing severe restrictions upon building of all kinds, it was unlikely that more than £20,000,000 of new building would be possible during the stated period. In the event, even this forecast proved over-optimistic; only £11,500,000 of new building had been completed by 1952.

Among this was some building for which money had been 'earmarked', that is, specially designated for particular projects. This practice of 'earmarking' had been usual before the war, on the rare occasions on which the Government had made grants to universities for capital expenditure. It was resumed in 1945, when the U.G.C. recommended that, in addition to the increased general grant, £1,000,000 be granted during each of the two years following the war for the development of medical education along the lines proposed by the Goodenough Committee and accepted by the Government. These 'earmarked' grants were made, and were followed by others; but, though individual 'earmarked' grants were welcome enough to their recipients, the principle of 'earmarking' was cordially disliked by the universities, on the grounds that it was liable to upset the balance of development. The U.G.C. equally disliked it, and were at pains to point out that they regarded it as a temporary expedient only, to be discarded at the earliest possible moment. 'Earmarking' was accordingly abandoned from 1947 onwards.

The delicate question of the relationship between the universities and the State in the new financial situation early engaged the anxious attention of both parties. The Government's decision in 1945 to double the annual grant for recurrent expenditure and to provide substantial grants for capital expenditure 'was rightly interpreted by the universities as initiating a new era in their financial relations with the State'.[1] Both the U.G.C. and the universities realised clearly that the implications of the new relationship were 'far-reaching and of profound importance', and in particular, that in the U.G.C.'s words[2] 'the question cannot be avoided whether the greatly increased dependence of the universities on Government grants may carry with it a threat to their continued existence as free institutions'.

It is impossible not to feel a vicarious pride about the entirely reasonable, and friendly, way in which this crucial question was handled. Both sides made concessions. The Committee of Vice-Chancellors and Principals, in *A Note on University Policy and Finance in the Decennium* 1947–56,[3] distributed in July 1946, agreed that:

> . . . the Universities entirely accept the view that the Government has not only the right but the duty to satisfy itself that every field of study which in the national interest ought to be cultivated in Great Britain is in fact being adequately cultivated in the University system and that the resources which are placed at the disposal of the Universities are being used with full regard both to efficiency and to economy.

The Vice-Chancellors very naturally believed that 'the Universities may properly be expected not only individually to make proper use of the resources entrusted to them, but collectively to devise and execute policies calculated to serve the national interest'; but they added that

> . . . in that task, both individually and collectively, they will be glad to have a greater measure of guidance from Government than until quite recent days they have been accustomed to receive.

Consequently, they said, they would be glad

> . . . if the University Grants Committee were formally authorised and equipped to undertake surveys of all the main fields of

---

[1] *University Development from* 1935 *to* 1947, p. 11.
[2] Ibid., p. 77.   [3] p. 14.

University activity designed to secure that as a whole the Universities are meeting the whole range of national need for higher teaching and research.

The new relationship was discussed at some length by the U.G.C. in their *Report on University Development from* 1935 *to* 1947.[1] The tenor of their advice about it to the Lords Commissioners of His Majesty's Treasury can, I think, be adequately illustrated by two short quotations from that Report. First:

> We are convinced that the road to an ordered plan of academic development is not that of dictation by an external authority, and we feel no doubt that the technique of informal consultation and discussion with the Committee of Vice-Chancellors and with representatives of individual universities on which we have mainly relied in the past is of equal applicability to the present situation (p. 78).

Secondly, after pointing out[2] that 'the character of the new and intricate relationship between the State and the universities . . . necessarily finds one of its expressions in the introduction of a certain measure of central planning', the Committee went on to assert that:

> . . . perhaps the most important of the functions to which we, as Your Lordships' advisers, are committed is that of devising appropriate means of reconciling the operation of planning with the maintenance of the essential academic freedoms.

'We are sustained in this task', the U.G.C. continued, 'by the conviction that the contrasting principles involved are not contradictory'. After examining these principles, they concluded that:

> Central planning on these lines involves no abridgment of academic freedom, for no university is required, or could be expected, to undertake developments against its own considered wishes. . . .

[1] See pp. 77–83.   [2] p. 81.

In the same month as the Vice-Chancellors issued their note on policy and finance the terms of reference of the U.G.C. were enlarged to meet the new situation. When the Committee was set up in 1919 its function was stated to be simply:

> To inquire into the financial needs of university education in the United Kingdom and to advise the Government as to the application of any grants that may be made towards meeting them.

The new terms of reference read:

> To inquire into the financial needs of university education in Great Britain;[1] to advise the Government as to the application of any grants made by Parliament towards meeting them; to collect, examine and make available information on matters relating to university education at home and abroad, and to assist, in consultation with the universities and other bodies concerned, the preparation and execution of such plans for the development of universities as may from time to time be required in order to ensure that they are fully adequate to national needs.

Except that in 1952 the requirement to collect and disseminate information from abroad was dropped, these terms of reference have remained unchanged up till the time of writing. There seems at present no likelihood that they will be altered.

This is not to say that everyone is completely happy about the financial relationship between the State and the universities. One body in particular, the Committee of Public Accounts of the House of Commons, has since 1948 repeatedly made clear that it is anything but happy about it. The core of the complaint made by this Committee, whose primary function is to check the legality of expenditures of public funds, is that:

> Parliament is entitled to expect assurances, based on some broad examination of the Universities' financial arrangements, that the grants are administered with due regard to economy.

[1] The Queen's University, Belfast, was excluded as being the concern of the Northern Ireland Government.

The information at present available to your Committee does not enable them to form an opinion on this question.[1]

In 1951–2 the Select Committee on Estimates of the House of Commons, after investigating the estimates for the quinquennial grant to the universities and university colleges for 1952–7, took a similar view.[2] Pointing out that 'this is by far the largest of the grants in aid of services at home of which detailed accounts are not available to the Comptroller and Auditor General' (it was in fact more than 100 times larger than any other), they recommended that:

(1) There should be inserted in the Estimates each year a note reconciling the amount of quinquennial grant proposed for the academic year with the total figure of recurrent grant shown in the Estimates for the financial year (para. 35);

(2) The fullest possible information should be supplied to Parliament, preferably in the Estimates, whenever changes in the amount of recurrent grants are made, either as a result of the quinquennial review or at other times, showing the reasons for the change and the basis on which it is calculated (para. 35);

(3) The practice, by which the books and accounts of bodies which receive the greater part of their income from public funds are normally open to inspection by the Comptroller and Auditor General, should be extended to cover all money advanced by means of non-recurrent grant to the Universities for capital development (para. 37).

The Treasury has throughout consistently opposed the introduction of any such control, on the general grounds that (a) every Government has rejected the idea that the State should control

[1] Committee of Public Accounts. Session 1950, Fourth Report, para. 40.

[2] Fifth Report from the Select Committee on Estimates. Session 1951–52. *The Grant in aid of Universities and Colleges.* H.M.S.O., 1952. The primary function of this Committee is to ensure that public funds voted by Parliament are efficiently and economically expended by their recipients.

academic policy, (b) any such detailed scrutiny of accounts would weaken the Universities' sense of responsibility, (c) only academics are capable of deciding what expenditure is or is not necessary for academic purposes, and (d) in any case the University Grants Committee undertakes such scrutiny, and does so in the capacity of an agent of the Treasury.

The last point was explicitly put to the Select Committee on Estimates in February 1952 by Mr E. W. Playfair, then a Third Secretary of the Treasury. Explaining, in the evidence he gave to the Committee, the difference between the Treasury's relations with the Ministry of Education and the U.G.C., he said:

> When we deal with, let us say, the Ministry of Education we are dealing either with the Accounting Officer or the Accountant-General there. We are dealing with a man who is a most trustworthy colleague, but who is a servant of another Minister and who is out to fight his battle and we fight by the Queensberry Rules, if necessary. *The situation is not quite the same with the University Grants Committee who are, in our minds, part of the Treasury. Their job is to do our job.* The Treasury is proud to call itself the friend of the learned institutions and tries to do its best for them, and it is there to look for rigorous economy, and the Committee do both parts. *Therefore we regard them as being our agents, and trustworthy agents, for all the detailed examination, and we do not put them through the same grilling which we do the Ministry of Education.*[1]

The Select Committee enquired very thoroughly into the control exercised by the U.G.C. over expenditure by universities. In the course of these enquiries the then Chairman of the U.G.C., the late Sir Arthur Trueman, agreed that the U.G.C.'s powers were 'very considerable', and when asked:

> Does the Committee take upon itself the authority to make representations to the universities that administrative costs or staffing or expenditure in other directions are of such an order that it would be much more satisfactory if alterations were made?

[1] *loc. cit.* Minutes of Evidence, p. 3. Italics mine.

he replied: 'We do indeed', and added that, on the Committee's visitations, after having seen the premises and talked with students, junior staff, members of the Senate and of the governing body:

> ... at the final meeting with the members of the governing body we always make opportunities to talk about the things in which we feel perhaps they have overspent or in which we think they ought to consider some revision.[1]

Though their demands were not conceded, the comments made by the Committee of Public Accounts and the Select Committee were not wholly without effect. In June 1954 the U.G.C. felt impelled to appoint a sub-committee, under the chairmanship of Sir George Gater:

> To report on the question whether, and if so what, changes are necessary to secure that universities' methods of contracting, and of recording and controlling expenditure from non-recurrent grants, are reasonably designed and properly applied to ensure effective safeguards against waste, extravagance, or other abuse.

The Gater Committee, which reported in January 1956, stated that 'they had found no evidence of a lack of appreciation of the need for economy in the expenditure of non-recurrent grants'.[2] But they did suggest a number of alterations in procedure which in total gave to the U.G.C. a considerably stricter control over such expenditure.

The Committee of Public Accounts returned repeatedly to the attack between 1950 and 1956. In their *Sixth Report*[3] they regretted that they were in no better position than were their predecessors to give an assurance that the non-recurrent grants made by Parliament to the universities had been spent on the purposes

[1] Ibid., p. 12.

[2] Quoted from *University Development. Interim Report on the Years 1952 to 1956.* University Grants Committee. Cmd. 79. H.M.S.O., p. 16.

[3] *Sixth Report from the Committee of Public Accounts,* Session 1955–6. H. C. 348. H.M.S.O.

for which they were voted and 'with due regard to the elimination of waste and extravagance'. They doubted whether the U.G.C. were in a position to satisfy themselves fully about these matters, and they expressed themselves as not satisfied that the U.G.C.'s control over the use of non-recurrent grants was as tight as might reasonably be expected. They reiterated the demand made previously that the Comptroller and Auditor-General should have access to the books and accounts of the universities, at least in respect of non-recurrent grants, and added:

> If the universities are spending their grants wisely they have nothing to fear, and they could be assured that it is not the practice or intention of the Comptroller and Auditor-General to raise questions of policy which might conflict in any way with their properly prized academic freedom.

To this Sir Eric Ashby, then President and Vice-Chancellor of the Queen's University, Belfast, replied, in an article in the *Universities Quarterly*:[1]

> . . . there already exists in the academic world a powerful and effective machinery for deciding whether money is being spent wisely, and (what is more important) a sound body of precedent as to what 'wisely' means . . . the Committee [of Public Accounts] is unwittingly attacking a most ingenious British social invention for supervising public expenditure on science and scholarship; the invention of appointing controllers who are drawn from the ranks of the controlled: scientists to administer grants for scientific research, medical men to administer grants for medical research, and academic men to administer grants to universities. It is assumed, and the assumption has been abundantly justified, that controllers of this calibre can determine, better than politicians or administrators can, the criteria for exercising control.

So far the view held by the Treasury and the Universities has prevailed. But it is far from certain that the last has been heard of this argument.

[1] November 1956, p. 10.

CHAPTER THREE

The period since the war has seen an expansion in the universities of this country at a rate to which no past period of the same duration affords a parallel. – UNIVERSITY GRANTS COMMITTEE.[1]

The increase in the number of students at British Universities began in earnest in 1946. The U.G.C. had tried, but without success, to bring it about earlier. In September 1944 they made a second approach to the Government, and received a favourable answer. The Government would consider applications for the early release of members of university staffs from the civil service, expedite the return of university buildings, and begin the release of students from the Forces for the academic year 1945–6.

The Government were as good as their word. In the academic year 1943–4 the number of full-time students at the universities had dropped from the pre-war 50,000 to 37,500; and even that figure concealed rather than disclosed the true position. The number of men had dropped by 41 per cent, and of men students of the Arts by 76 per cent; and of those who were then up at the university many were doing shortened courses. During the academic year 1945–6 men and women from the Forces entered the British universities in such a flood that the total number of students exceeded the pre-war peak of rather more than 50,000. During the following four years the numbers rose spectacularly, as under:

1946–47		63,000
1947–48	(almost)	77,000
1948–49		83,690
1949–50		85,421

[1] *University Development: Report on the years 1947 to 1952.* H.M.S.O., 1953, p. 11.

Throughout these years a large proportion of the students were ex-service men and women; at the beginning of the 1947–8 session, for example, these numbered 28,122 (26,291 men and 1,831 women), that is, well over one-third of the student population. So long as this state of affairs lasted, the expansion was, in character, very similar to that which took place after the 1914–18 war, though the earlier expansion was both swifter and proportionately larger; as early as 1920–1 the number of full-time students (48,452) was more than double the number (23,872) in 1913–14.

In both periods it was anticipated that as the ex-service students completed their courses the total number of students would decline. In both cases this happened, but there was a significant difference between the two declinations. In the 1920s the decrease amounted (in 1925–6, the lowest year) to over 14 per cent; in the 1950s it was never lower than $5\frac{1}{2}$ per cent. And, when the numbers began to rise again, as they did in both cases, there was an equally significant difference.

The decline in the 1950s persisted for four years only; the figures were:

1950–1	85,314
1951–2	83,458
1952–3	81,474
1953–4	80,602

In the late 1920s and early 1930s the numbers rose steadily but only slightly; then in 1933–4 the tide turned, and from 1934–5 onwards they decreased. There seems no reason to believe that, even had war not broken out in 1939, they would not have continued to do so. From 1954–5 the numbers have risen with increasing momentum, and there is as yet no indication that a final limit is in sight. On the contrary, the Government have since 1956 raised the target three times: in November of that year to 106,000 by the mid-1960s, in February 1958 to 124,000 by that time, with a possible increase to 136,000 by 1970, and in January 1960 to 170,000 or 175,000 by the early 1970s at the latest. And competent judges are already talking of an ultimate university student population of 200,000 or more. The totals so far are as under:

1954–5	81,705
1955–6	85,194
1956–7	89,866
1957–8	95,442
1958–9	100,204
1959–60	102,000 (approx.)

This continued, and accelerating, increase owes as yet (1960) nothing to the famous 'bulge', the large increase in the birthrate during the late 1940s which has for years sorely troubled the primary and secondary schools. That will not hit the universities with full force until about 1962. The increases of the past five years have been made possible by two dissimilar but related phenomena: a progressive growth in the numbers of pupils remaining at school until the age of 17 or over, and a huge, and equally progressive, growth in the number of awards made from public funds to enable students to undertake university education. The fundamental cause of both these phenomena is the nation's realisation that its future prosperity, and status as a world power, depend upon its producing a large, and increasing, number of highly educated and professionally trained men and women: chiefly, but far from exclusively, scientists and technologists. In short, university education has become a national investment, and the Government are determining the size of the investment.

That being so, it is pertinent to examine rather more closely the size, the pace and the nature of this post-1945 expansion. It has frequently – not to say monotonously – been described as 'unprecedented'. Is it this, and if so, in what respects?

It is perhaps not out of order to begin by saying that the same epithet, 'unprecedented', was also applied to both the expansion between 1900 and 1914 and that which occurred after 1918. As has been shown, the rise in the number of students in the early 1920s was swifter and proportionately larger than that which took place in the 1940s. Here I wish to examine the matter in a longer historical perspective. Since the circumstances are somewhat different in Scotland I am confining my analysis to England and Wales.

In 1815 there are said to have been about 2,000 students at Oxford and Cambridge, then the only English universities. In 1914 there were in the universities and university colleges of England and Wales about 18,000 full-time students, that is, about nine times as many. Had this increase been spread evenly over the decades it would have represented a rise of approximately 25 per cent in every ten years, or in other words a doubling of the number of students every thirty years or so. In fact, the increase was very largely concentrated within the last quarter of the nineteenth century and the first decade of the twentieth, the period during which the university colleges were growing up and achieving university status. For example, between 1896 and 1906 the number of day students at Liverpool rose from about 475 to 785, and at Sheffield from about 245 to about 495.

During the years between the two world wars the average rate of increase was greater; the number of students was doubled in the twenty years between 1918 and 1938. But this increase was spread most unevenly over these years; as has been shown, it took place almost entirely between 1920 and 1926. In the 1930s there was a net increase of only about 1,000.

Since the second world war the number of university students in Great Britain has been almost exactly doubled in fourteen years. This denotes a marked quickening of the tempo of increase, but by itself hardly justifies the use of the word 'unprecedented'. Still less justified is the U.G.C.'s statement, quoted at the head of this chapter, that the expansion up to 1952 had been 'at a rate to which no past period of the same duration affords a parallel'; as has been shown, by 1920–1 the number of students was well over double the number in 1913–14. Reasons for using the words 'unprecedented' must be sought elsewhere than in the rate of increase and the proportionate growth of student numbers.

The first is that, as has been pointed out, the present expansion is still continuing, and with growing momentum. The second, that the increase in numbers has been spread much more unevenly over the universities than ever before. There has always been a tendency for the larger, and older-established, institutions to expand less than the smaller and younger; but the contrast has never before been anything like so striking. Up to the academic year 1957–8 none of the three largest universities, London, Cambridge, and Oxford, had so much as doubled in size (and the Oxford numbers actually decreased in the following year). On the other hand, the 'modern' universities showed a collective increase during the same period of nearly 300 per cent. But even among this group of universities growth had been most unevenly spread, and again, with one or two exceptions, it was the larger and older institutions that had made the smaller proportionate increases. Manchester, for example, the largest university after Oxford, Cambridge and London, had increased by only about 130 per cent (2,462 to 5,636), even when the affiliation of the Manchester College of Science and Technology (in 1956) is taken into account. Liverpool, the next largest, had not by 1957–8 even doubled its numbers. But Nottingham, which in 1938–9 was a university college of 582 students, had more than quadrupled its numbers (to 2,337), and Sheffield was well over three times as large as in 1938–9 (767 to 2,491).

The most spectacular increases, however, had taken place at the two university colleges, Hull and Leicester, which were first recognised for grant by the U.G.C. in 1945. By 1957–8 – within a dozen years – the number of students at Hull had increased by over 800 per cent (162 to 1,303), and at Leicester by over 1,100 per cent (82 to 925). That quality had not been sacrificed to quantity is evidenced by the fact that towards the end of this period both colleges received Charters conferring on them full university status: Hull in 1954 and Leicester in 1957.

This pattern of expansion has produced two effects to which perhaps insufficient attention has yet been paid. First, the facilities for university education are today much more evenly distributed over England and Wales than they were before the war. Secondly, the numerical preponderance of Oxford, Cambridge, and London has been greatly diminished. In 1938–9 these three universities contained nearly two-thirds of the student population of England and Wales (24,145 out of 39,212); by 1957–8 the proportion had dropped to well under half (37,271 out of 79,031). Redbrick had become numerically the dominant element in English university education. This trend continues.

In the realm of qualitative change three features are outstanding. First, in 1938–9 about 40 per cent of students in the universities of England and Wales were receiving financial assistance from public or private funds. By 1957–8 the proportion had been more than doubled; in England 80·9 per cent, and in Wales 92·2 per cent, of students were being financially assisted, the overwhelming majority of them in whole or in part from public funds. Numerically, this expansion of aid from public funds could, like the expansion of student numbers, be regarded as no more than an acceleration of an evolutionary process, for the proportion of university students thus assisted had been growing steadily throughout the twentieth century. But, as well as becoming far more numerous, the grants, though still determined by a parental means test, had also become far more generous, amounting in the case of many students to full maintenance; and they had been differentiated to meet the different scales of expenditure demanded by different universities and by residence in college or hall of residence, lodgings, or at home.

By far the most important result of this is, as is well known, that today very large numbers of students come from homes which never before aspired to university education for any of their members. But the effects upon the universities should not be overlooked. One only will be mentioned at this juncture. Since students are no longer compelled by financial considerations, as they so frequently were in the past, to attend the university nearest to their home, the modern universities have become far less 'civic', or even 'provincial', and far more 'national' than ever before. The decrease in the proportion of students living at home has been constant and striking. In 1938–9, 41·7 per cent of all full-time university students in Great Britain lived at home. By 1957–8 the proportion had dropped to 25·2 per cent, and this despite the fact that in Scotland over half, and in London nearly one-third, of the students resided at home. In 1958–9 it was only 23·8 per cent.

The removal of the financial inducement to attend the local university has had another, very different, consequence, which many people, both in and outside university work, deplore. Since it is now financially as easy to attain one university as any other, the prestige, and other advantages they can offer, of Oxford and Cambridge, and to a lesser degree of London, act as an irresistible magnet to a large majority of potential university students, and (probably more importantly) to the secondary school heads and teachers who guide their steps towards the university. There is no doubt that these three Universities, and more particularly Oxford and Cambridge, skim off the richest cream of the intellectual ability of each annual tally of applicants to enter universities.

There is nothing new in this except the scale on which it is happening. Throughout the lives of the modern universities Oxford, Cambridge, and London have diverted from them many – perhaps the majority – of the ablest minds among both students and staff. But though it cannot be measured, there can be little doubt that since 1945 the trend, in respect of students at any rate, has become very much stronger. As a result, there is reason to fear that, except in departments unique to modern universities, such as, for example, malting and brewing at Birmingham, textile industries at Leeds, and glass technology at Sheffield, or other departments, mainly technological, which have achieved outstanding reputations, the general level of intellectual ability among undergraduate students at the modern universities is lower than at the two ancient universities and London.

The third change is that throughout the period the centre of gravity in university studies has been shifting, as the result of deliberate national policy, from the arts to the sciences and technology. The comparative percentages for 1938–9 and 1957–8 are as shown in the first table on the opposite page:[1]

It will be seen, however, that despite persistent and intensive national propaganda for more scientists and technologists, and the heavy emphasis in Government building policy upon facilities for teaching pure and applied sciences, the arts subjects have all but

[1] Taken from *Returns from Universities and University Colleges,* 1957–58. (Cmd. 832) U.G.C. H.M.S.O., 1959, p. 7.

FULL-TIME STUDENTS OTHER THAN THOSE DOING ADVANCED WORK

Subjects	Percentage of total		Gain or loss
	1938–9	1957–8	
Arts	45·2	42·0	−3·2
Pure Science	13·6	21·9	+8·3
Technology	10·4	14·7	+4·3
Medicine	24·9	14·4	−10·5
Dentistry	3·2	3·5	+0·3
Agriculture	2·1	2·1	—
Veterinary Science	0·6	1·4	+0·8

held their ground. Nor is this due, as some people seem to imagine, to the fact that most women students choose these subjects. They do; but the comparative percentages of decline[1] are not significantly different for men and women.

ARTS SUBJECTS

Per cent of men		Per cent of women	
1938–9	1957–8	1938–9	1957–8
38·7	36·4	64·7	63·5

An unanswered, and perhaps unanswerable, question is whether the intellectual quality of the students on the arts side has declined. No statistics can answer this, not even comparative lists of classes gained in degree examinations, or of the proportionate numbers of students securing honours and pass degrees, because

[1] Ibid.

no one has yet devised a technique that will measure the intellectual calibre, and other qualities, required for passing degree examinations in different subjects. And even were such a technique discovered, there would still remain to be assessed such imponderables as the quality of the teaching a student receives, and the conditions in which his teaching and learning have to be done. Whilst not suggesting that any certain conclusions can be drawn, it seems reasonable to suspect that it is considerably easier to teach and to learn in the fine, modernly equipped laboratories and workshops that have been provided in so many universities for the sciences and the technologies than in the scrubby and overcrowded little villas in which, alas, so many arts departments have still to attempt to pursue their studies.

All one can say about this question is that there appears to be a widespread impression among university teachers, and among heads of secondary schools sending pupils to the university, that the balance of ability as well as of numbers is moving from the arts to the sciences and technologies, and that as a consequence the average level of intellectual ability among students of the arts is already lower than it was before the war.

It will be seen from the table on page 97 that the largest percentage gain has been made by Pure Science. This is because the number of girls, as well as of boys, taking subjects under this head has increased. The comparative percentages are:

PURE SCIENCES

Per cent of men		Per cent of women	
1938–9	1957–8	1938–9	1957–8
15·2	23·7	15·9	20·0

In the technologies the case is far different; the percentage of women has remained precisely the same – though the actual number has, of course, increased.

APPLIED SCIENCES

Per cent of men		Per cent of women	
1938–9	1957–8	1938–9	1957–8
13·5	19·0	0·8	0·8

The increase in the number of men studying technological subjects, while substantial, has not satisfied either hopes or expectations. It will be seen that the percentage gain is considerably below that for Pure Science. For this lag there appears to be a disposition, among some university teachers of the applied sciences at least, to blame the secondary schools. If I might venture – perhaps presumptuously – to offer an opinion, this criticism is only partially justified. Among both teachers and practitioners of the technologies it is agreed that for all technologies a sound basic knowledge of mathematics and physics, and in some cases of chemistry as well, is absolutely essential. The proper task of the secondary schools, therefore, is to concentrate on these basic subjects, as they do. What is wanted is for more university teachers to come and talk to Sixth Forms about their particular technologies, many of which are but names (if as much as that) to most Sixth Form pupils – and, often, to their teachers.

The large fall in the proportionate number of medical students is the direct result of Government policy. The Goodenough Committee asked for only a relatively small increase in the total number of students. Twelve years later unease about the possibility of over-production of doctors resulted in the recommendation by a committee (Chairman, Sir Henry Willink) set up to investigate the position that there should be a temporary reduction of 10 per cent in the intake into medical schools. The very small increase in the proportionate number of entrants into the dental schools was probably partly due to disinclination to enter the profession of dentistry. (By 1960 this trend had been reversed; there

were far more applicants than places in the dental schools.)
Agriculture only just succeeded in holding its own, despite the
acquisition in 1947 by Nottingham University College (as it then
was) of the Midland Agricultural College at Sutton Bonington, the
amalgamation in 1948 of the South Eastern Agricultural College,
Wye, and the Horticultural College for Women at Swanley, as a
constituent college of the University of London, and the establishment in 1947 at King's College, Newcastle-upon-Tyne (University
of Durham) of a professorial chair in Agricultural Engineering –
the first in the country. The large proportionate rise in the number
of veterinary students does not in fact represent a large increase
of students. It was due to the incorporation (on the recommendation of the Inter-Departmental Committee on Veterinary Education in Great Britain) of non-university schools at London,
Edinburgh and Glasgow in the universities.

Altogether, the relative numbers of students in the different
Faculties have not altered so largely as many people expected, or
perhaps Government policy has intended. Somewhat surprisingly,
this is even more true of post-graduate than of first-degree
students, as the following table shows.[1] (The figures do not

POST-GRADUATE STUDENTS

Subjects	Percentage of total		Gain or loss
	1938–9	1957–8	
Arts	38·0	35·3	−2·7
Pure Science	41·0	34·8	−6·2
Technology	12·5	17·3	+4·8
Medicine	6·4	8·8	+2·4
Dentistry	—	0·4	+0·4
Agriculture	2·1	2·8	+0·7
Veterinary Science	—	0·6	+0·6

[1] Figures from *Returns from Universities and University Colleges*,
1957–8.

include post-graduates taking courses leading to a teacher's Certificate or Diploma.)

The comparatively slight changes shown in the above table become even more surprising when it is learned that the total proportion of students doing advanced work other than teacher training has very considerably increased since the war. In 1937–8 (I have not been able to find the figures for 1938–9), of a total of 49,189 full-time students 3,021 were doing advanced work, that is, slightly over one in 16. In 1957–8, of 98,442 full-time students 11,062, or more than one in nine, were engaged in advanced work. Among part-time students the change was even more striking. In 1937–8, of 13,081 part-time students 1,992, or approximately one in 6·5, were doing advanced work; in 1957–8 there were 5,446 out of 16,486, or almost one in three. In view of the intense and persistent pressure for more highly qualified scientists and technologists the proportionate increases of students in these disciplines can only be regarded as disappointing.

Summing up, one can agree that the present expansion of the universities is unprecedented. But it is unprecedented, not because either the rate of increase or the proportionate growth of student numbers (up to 1960) is unparalleled. It is unprecedented first, because after a decade and a half numbers continue to increase; secondly, because the social character of the student population is being, by design, radically altered; thirdly, because the balance between the humanities and the sciences is being deliberately shifted; and finally, because all this is due to accept-ance of the doctrine that university education has become a national investment, and that consequently State subsidies to the universities are no longer to be regarded as a supplement to their private funds but as their principal means of support. The implementation of this doctrine will be examined in the next chapter.

CHAPTER FOUR

But large though this increase is the Government believe that the universities should be encouraged to expand even more . . . to meet national needs. – MR HENRY BROOKE, Financial Secretary to the Treasury.[1]

It has been shown that the rate of increase in the number of students since 1945 is not without precedent. Nor for that matter is the rate of increase in the amount of recurrent grants. The average rate of grant announced for the quinquennium 1957–62 (the annual grants are, as previously, on a rising scale: from £30,600,000 in 1957–8 to £39,500,000 in 1961–2) is approximately sixteen times as large as the recurrent grant made in 1938–9, even when a small supplementary grant made in 1958 is included. But, as everyone knows, the real value of money has dropped tremendously since 1939. So, while it is impossible to make anything like an exact comparison, it seems safe to suggest that the annual grants for 1957–62 are not, in terms of purchasing power, more than five to ten times as large as the grant for 1938–9. But in the ten years preceding the first World War the recurrent grants made by the Treasury to Universities and Colleges were increased over sixteen-fold: from £27,000 in 1903–4 to £442,000 in 1913–14, in a period when the value of money was relatively stable. Even during the inter-war years, an era of financial crises, large-scale unemployment, and consequent stringent governmental economy, the recurrent Treasury grants were more than trebled in value: from £790,000 in 1919–20 to £2,400,000 in 1938–9. Or, if one wishes to rub the point home by making comparison with the

[1] In the House of Commons, November 21st, 1956, as reported in *The Times Educational Supplement*, November 23rd, 1956, p. 1380.

1913—14 figure (and thus making the comparison with the period 1938—62 more exact), the grant was increased almost sixfold

Regretfully, it has to be said not only that the rate of increase of the recurrent grants since 1945 is not unprecedented, but also that relatively the country has done better in the past. Admittedly, these comparisons I have made are crude, and account ought to be taken of a wide variety of circumstances before anything in the nature of an indictment of Government policy since 1945 is built up on them; for instance, it should be remembered that between 1903 and 1914 Britain was an immensely wealthy country, and that in addition university grants could be made out of a national revenue upon which only very slight demands were made for social welfare provision. Nevertheless, the comparisons stand, and in view of the fact that the basis upon which recurrent grants are now made – that they are the main source of the universities' income, and not merely a supplement – implies a totally different scale of Government subvention, one is bound to wonder whether any post-war Government have realised the full implications of their changed policy. Certainly, one can appreciate and sympathise with the universities' complaints, made every time a new scale of recurrent grants has been announced, that the grants are seriously inadequate. The universities have expanded, time and again, at the Government's request, in many individual instances against their own inclinations; they are undertaking, for the same reason, still further expansions; and there is no certainty that they will not be asked – indeed, it is very likely that they will – to revise upwards the estimates of student numbers to which they are now working.

When one looks at non-recurrent grants for capital expenditure a very different picture is revealed. I have not been able to discover how much of the Treasury grants made up to 1914 went on capital expenditure; but the total sum could not have been very considerable. Apart from the fact that the Treasury in 1908 laid down the principle that their grants were for maintenance rather than capital expenditure (and probably worked to it long before), the grants were, until 1905, so small as to permit of little or nothing in the way of large-scale building.

Between 1919 and 1939 there are official figures for non-recurrent Treasury grants. In those twenty years grants amounting to slightly over £1,500,000 were made for capital expenditure. But of that sum almost £900,000 was allocated in the three years 1919–22. In only two of the subsequent sixteen years did the total of the non-recurrent grants exceed £100,000, and in six of the years no such grants were made at all.

Between 1947 and 1959 non-recurrent Treasury grants amounting to over £80,000,000 were made, and the annual totals rose progressively, from about £2,150,000 in 1947—8 to £12,000,000 in 1958–9. Another £12,000,000 is promised for 1959–60,[1] and for the following four years a total of £60,000,000, or an average of £15,000,000 a year.

Here is clear recognition of the implications of the new policy. Though private benefaction is still playing a part in university building, this has become a very minor part. In effect, the Government is paying for the new and enlarged buildings which the universities must have in order to undertake the expansions which the Government have requested them to make. That being so, two crucial questions must be asked. Is sufficient money being provided to meet the universities' needs, and is the universities' autonomy being infringed by their almost complete dependence upon the Government for money for capital expenditure?

It seems fairly safe to say that the universities' unanimous answer to the first question would be No, though it must be added that some, at least, were not entirely dissatisfied with the amount they were allocated under the Government's £60,000,000 four-year plan for 1960–3. But about previous allocations, especially the earlier ones, the opinion expressed by Sir James Mountford, Vice-Chancellor of Liverpool University, in 1955[2] would probably be echoed by all the universities. Addressing the University Court, Sir James Mountford said:

[1] The sums for 1957–9 are exclusive of the cost of capital expenditure upon the enlargement of the Imperial College of Science and Technology, London.

[2] As reported in *The Times Educational Supplement* on December 2nd, 1955.

The one thing in which we have been starved has been the provision of buildings in which to carry on our work. In this matter experience during the last ten years has been one of continuous disappointment and frustration; and within the foreseeable future, unless drastic action is taken now, the situation for the universities will become unmanageable and from a national point of view quite disastrous.

The second question is much more difficult to answer. On the one hand, the U.G.C. took an early opportunity[1] to say quite definitely that:

Central planning on these lines involves no abridgment of academic freedom, for no university is required, or could be expected, to undertake developments against its own considered wishes . . .

But the Committee went on to say[2] that:

if a university feels impelled to expenditure on purposes for which financial support from the Exchequer is not forthcoming, its remedy is to find a private benefactor to supply the need.

And there's the rub. What university is going to refuse the offer of a fine new engineering building, immediately, and cost free to itself, even if it knows that its really urgent need is for a new arts building or a Students' Union – for which no 'financial support from the Exchequer' is likely to be forthcoming for years, while the chance of an adequate donation from a 'private benefactor' is so slight as to be practically negligible ?[3]

In *University Development* 1952–7 there is a list[4] of ninety-six major building projects for which starts had been approved during that quinquennium. Of these, fifty are for science or technology

[1] In *University Development from 1935 to 1947*, p. 81.
[2] Ibid., pp. 81–2.
[3] Though such gifts are not unknown even today, as witness the £250,000 given in 1957 to London University by the Isaac Wolfson Trust to build a hall of residence for Commonwealth students.
[4] Appendix VIII, pp. 86–88.

(excluding medicine and veterinary science). The nearest competitor is halls of residence for students, nine projects for which were approved. Only five projects were for buildings for the teaching of the humanities, and only seven for libraries. The need for more and bigger buildings for the teaching of scientific and technological subjects is undoubted, and for years to come such buildings will form the major part of any university building programme. But it is impossible to believe that the needs of the universities for arts buildings, libraries, and halls of residence (about which I shall have more to say in Part III) are so slight as is suggested by that 1952–7 list – which is closely paralleled by other such lists of building projects. The plain fact is that the Government's – every Government's – financial policy is dictating the shape of the universities and the place which the various disciplines will occupy in them. The universities have really only one area of choice: whether to make acceptable proposals, and so expand, and grow in reputation, or to accept the fact that they will be supported only at subsistence level. In saying this I am not questioning the wisdom of a policy of heavy concentration upon the teaching of scientific and technological subjects, or suggesting that the universities have co-operated unwillingly in forwarding that policy. They have not; but it is no secret that many, if not all, would have liked to have other buildings as well, but could not, because financial support from the Exchequer was not forthcoming for them.

The post-war governmental attitude towards the provision of public funds for capital expenditure by the universities is without precedent; and it has brought about an almost complete reversal of previous policy. Up to the time of writing (June 1960) the attitude towards the provision of financial assistance to university (and other) students, though far more openhanded than before the war, has remained essentially the same. Consequently, there has been no reversal of policy; grants from public funds to students (except post-graduate students) are still a supplement to private resources. This is a continuation of pre-war policy.

For many years before 1945 it had been the Government's policy – a policy sanctioned by a centuries-old British tradition –

to make grants-in-aid to poor but able children to assist them to undertake a university education. In the present century the practice was begun by local authorities (whose expenditure was grant-aided by the Government), and by 1911 they were providing, in England and Wales, some 1,400 scholarships at universities and university colleges. In that year the Board of Education took a direct hand by offering university scholarships to intending teachers. In 1920 the Board made a new departure; they began to offer annually, to secondary school pupils in England and Wales,[1] 200 'State Scholarships', free of any commitment to enter the teaching profession. In 1930 the number of State Scholarships was raised to 300 a year, and in 1936 to 360. By that time the English local education authorities were offering each year rather more than 1,500 scholarships and awards.

What has been done since 1945 has been to broaden and strengthen this 'ladder of opportunity' to such an extent that it has become rather a highway along which many may travel than a ladder up which a few may climb.

In 1931 Professor E. R. Dodds wrote, rather sadly, in the *Universities Review*[2]:

> The most obvious (though happily not the only) function which these [i.e., the modern] universities today discharge is that of a social ladder. They do not exist for the education of the 'working classes'; if they did, they would be almost empty. It would be truer (though not entirely true) to say that they exist to enable certain members of the working classes to escape from their class by becoming schoolmasters and schoolmistresses.

That is no longer true. All the universities, Oxbridge type as well as Redbrick, are open to children of ability, irrespective of class or financial circumstances. It would be possible today for a British university to be entirely filled with sons and daughters of the 'working classes' – or, for that matter, with the sons and daughters of unemployed or pauper parents. This state of affairs

[1] The State Scholarship System has never been adopted in Scotland·
[2] In an article entitled 'What is wrong with the Modern Universities'? October 1931.

has only come about by stages. In 1946 the previous limit of £100 a year for the maintenance of State Scholars was abolished, and it was agreed that where necessary the full standard rate of maintenance would be paid by the Minister of Education. At the same time the Minister also agreed to supplement the amounts gained by winners of open scholarships or other awards offered by universities, since these amounts were almost all much too small to provide full maintenance. Subject to certain conditions about the titular value of these awards, and the academic standards demanded to secure them, the supplement would place their holders on the same financial level as State Scholars.

The number of State Scholarships offered yearly was increased in 1947 to 750, in 1948 to 800, in 1949 to 1,050, and in 1951 to 2,000. From 1947 a few (at first 20, and later 30) of these scholarships were reserved for candidates aged 25 and upwards, and a rather larger number (at first 100, and later increased by stages to 225 a year) for students from technical colleges and other establishments of Further Education. Meanwhile the number of awards made by local education authorities has increased every year, and at the time of writing stands at about 18,700 annually (16,700 in England and Wales, 2,000 in Scotland[1]). In the earlier post-war years the value of L.E.A. awards varied widely in different areas, and many of the awards were 'minor awards', that is, worth only small sums quite inadequate to maintain students. But persistent pressure by the Minister of Education, and the example of the more generous L.E.A.s, have almost eliminated the minor awards, and though discrepancies still exist in the value of major awards, and in the proportionate number offered by L.E.A.s, these are far slighter than they used to be.

In addition to the awards offered by the Minister and the L.E.A.s a considerable number is now made by industrial organisations. The National Coal Board offers the largest number; since 1947 it has been prepared to give up to 100 scholarships a year. Most, if not all, of the industrial awards carry full mainten-

[1] In Scotland almost all the awards are made by the L.E.A.s Since the war increases in number and value broadly comparable with those in England have been made.

ance, and are made irrespective of the financial circumstances of the scholarship holder's parents. This is not the case with the awards made by the public authorities, all of which, with the exception of those made for post-graduate study or research (which are not included in the figures given above), are subject to a parental means test. This test has all along been the cause of much controversy, and of anxiety, and all too frequently of sacrifice, on the part of the parents, but according to the law as it stands at present it must be imposed. The Sections of the Education Act, 1944, numbers 81 and 100, which empower the L.E.A.s and the Minister to make grants for higher education, specifically state that such grants are to be made 'for the purpose of enabling pupils to take advantage without hardship to themselves or their parents of any educational facilities available to them'. There is no obligation upon the public authorities to provide full maintenance except in the case of students whose parents would be unable without hardship to contribute anything.

Many people (and I am one) have long regarded this system as both unsatisfactory and anomalous. The principle of the means test was upheld by a Working Party[1] appointed by the Minister of Education in 1948. Nevertheless, public agitation for its abandonment persisted, and in 1958 the Minister of Education and the Secretary of State for Scotland appointed a committee (Chairman, Sir Colin Anderson):

To consider the present system of awards from public funds to students attending first degree courses at universities and comparable courses at other institutions and to make recommendations.

The committee reported in May 1960. Eleven of the the fifteen members recommended:[2]

. . . that parental contributions should be abolished and that parents of students receiving awards from public funds should not be eligible for the income tax or surtax child allowances for those students.

[1] *University Awards*, H.M.S.O., 1948, p. 18.
[2] *Grants to Students* (Cmd. 1051), H.M.S.O., 1960, p. 59.

The Government were not prepared immediately to go so far as that, though they did not rule out abolition 'if', as the Minister of Education told Parliament, 'after consideration it should turn out to be the right thing to do'. The main difficulty was that 'whatever we do for university students we must do for all other full-time students in higher education'. The Government did not know how many such students there should be; they would therefore make a comprehensive study of the future of higher education in England and Wales. The question of abolition of the 'means test' would be included in that study.

In December 1960 the Minister announced a revised scale of parental contributions, applicable not only to university students but also to students taking comparable courses in further education institutions and teachers in training. No contribution would be required from parents with a net 'scale' income below £700 a year, and substantial reductions would be made in the amounts which parents with larger incomes would have to contribute. The income tax child allowance would be continued.

This revision is clearly an interim measure. It will bring substantial relief to many thousands of parents. Some 10,000 additional families, the Minister estimated, would have no contribution to pay, and the percentage of students on full grants would rise from 25 to 40. But the revision implies no change of governmental policy. The question of whether or not university education in Great Britain is to be regarded as primarily a national investment has again been side-stepped. Sooner or later a decision must be made on that fundamental issue; and in my opinion all the signs suggest that it should be sooner rather than later.

CHAPTER FIVE

Most students go through our universities without ever having been forced to exercise their minds on the issues which are really momentous.
– SIR WALTER MOBERLY.[1]

The material aspects of university expansion have, very naturally, absorbed so much of the attention of everyone concerned that all too little energy has been left over for consideration of the fundamental educational and social problems which are always inherent in university education, and assume particular importance in times of rapid growth and development. It is greatly to the credit of the U.G.C. that they have never allowed themselves to be entirely preoccupied with questions of finance, buildings, and numbers, but have always devoted a part of each of their quinquennial reports to discussing one or more of these deeper problems.

While there has been a considerable, though not large, output of newspaper and periodical articles about such problems, the number of books devoted to them has been disappointingly small. One can, in fact, count them on the fingers of one hand. But among this small number there are one or two which are outstanding.

In 1940 Professor Adolf Löwe, then at Manchester University, published a slim volume entitled *The Universities in Transformation*.[2] In this he maintained that the 'happy synthesis' which had existed in the education of the 'ruling type' at Oxford and Cambridge during the latter part of the nineteenth century had broken down, to be replaced by a lack of harmony between the universities and society, due to 'change in the general social

[1] *Crisis in the University*, S.C.M. Press, 1949, p. 70.
[2] Sheldon Press, London: Macmillan, New York.

background'. The task facing the universities was to learn how to educate, not the 'ruling type', but what he called 'social function-aries', the 'enlightened experts' who would be the architects and administrators of a planned society.

In 1943 a pseudonymous author who called himself 'Bruce Truscot' dropped the equivalent of a high-explosive bomb into the academic world (and its blast stunned many outside it) in the shape of a book entitled *Redbrick University*.[1] As was revealed after his death, the pseudonym concealed the lively personality of Professor E. Allison Peers, Professor of Spanish at Liverpool University; but during his lifetime only half-a-dozen persons (of whom I was privileged to be one) knew who 'Bruce Truscot' was. In a sense this secrecy, which Peers went to extraordinary lengths to preserve, was unfortunate, because it meant that a very great deal of academic energy went into trying to penetrate it which might better have been devoted to discussion of the contents of his book, some of which were revolutionary and almost all provocative.

Truscot's principal theme was the nature and functions of a university. About this he had clear and inflexible views. 'A university', he wrote,[2] 'is a corporation or society which devotes itself to a search after knowledge for the sake of its intrinsic value'. A university had two aims: research and teaching; but, said he,[3] 'the primary aim of the university must be search for knowledge – re-search, as we call it today'. In support of this claim he penned the famous, and oft-quoted, passage[4] which reads:

... to the idea of a university only the 'Fellows', the researchers, are essential. There could perfectly well be a university which, like All Souls College, Oxford, had no undergraduates at all; and, instead of teaching, replenished its ranks by the choice of scholars who had been taught elsewhere, devoting itself entirely and exclusively to the pursuit of knowledge. But there could never be a university which had no researchers at all and

[1] Faber, 1943.
[2] *Redbrick University*, p. 45.   [4] Ibid., p. 49.
[3] Ibid., p. 48.

which engaged in nothing but teaching . . . A university without research would be nothing but a super-secondary school.

The first part of that quotation represents an extreme point of view. Truscot adhered to it passionately; he assured me vehemently that he was not exaggerating for the sake of emphasis when he wrote it. The primacy of 'the search after knowledge' was to him 'a basic article of faith'. But, far from denying that the university had a teaching function, he held that this was 'a natural development from the essential idea of the university'. The seekers after truth, the researchers, could not be content with discovery. They were also impelled to disseminate knowledge, and not merely by writing books, but also 'through living channels'. So,

> they seek contact with others, especially with the young, who are like-minded with themselves, and train them, first and foremost, to be discoverers of fresh knowledge – i.e., researchers – and secondarily, to be diffusers of the knowledge which they give them as part of their self-imposed task.[1]

It is a beautiful ideal; but it has little relation to the reality of today.

It must be added that Truscot's definition of 'research'[2] was a far broader one than probably most academics would accept; in fact, many of them might very likely consider it rather a definition of scholarship. Truscot was well aware of this; he prefaced his definition (given under) by saying that, even omitting 'one important aspect of it – the stimulation of the spirit of research in the undergraduate – it will be much wider than any commonly envisaged'.

> First, it will comprise all original work of a scholarly kind, such as investigation, criticism, the intelligent publication of texts, appreciation based on scholarship, and certain types of imaginative and creative ability. It will, of course, include the presentation of facts or ideas either in a new light or (as a rule) in such a way as to bring them within the reach of those from whom they would otherwise be excluded. It can further be extended

[1] p. 48.   [2] p. 112.

to the keeping abreast of contemporary investigation and thought in one's own field and to a critical receptiveness of new ideas in that field or in any other which one may have studied. Finally, it takes in, not only the pursuit of all these activities oneself, but the encouraging, stimulating and training of others to pursue them, and participation in the activities of bodies devoted to their furtherance.

Two years after the publication of *Redbrick University* there appeared in Britain a book expressing a directly contrary view about the functions of a university. This was *Mission of the University*,[1] by the Spanish thinker José Ortega y Gasset, first published in 1930. To Gasset the university was (or ought to be) 'the projection of the student to the scale of an institution',[2] and its duty was to teach 'the ordinary student to be a cultured person and a good member of a profession'.[3] He regarded the 'trend towards a university dominated by "inquiry"' as 'disastrous'.[4] One of the baneful results of this trend, he declared,[5] had been 'the awarding of professorships, in keeping with the mania of the times, to research workers who are nearly always very poor professors, and regard their teaching as time stolen away from their work in the laboratory or the archives'. This was all wrong, thought Gasset. In his opinion: 'The selection of professors will depend not on their rank as investigators but on their talent for synthesis and their gift for teaching'. But even the aim of the teaching had become perverted. Gasset's central theme was that 'We cannot live on the human level without ideas', and that it was culture, which to him meant 'the *vital* system of ideas of a period', which was 'what saves human life from being a disaster'. The primary function of the university, therefore, was to preserve, enrich, and inculcate culture. But this the university was not doing:

. . . compared with the medieval university, the contemporary university has developed the mere seed of professional instruc-

[1] Translated by Howard Lee Nostrand. Routledge & Kegan Paul, 1944.   [2] p. 70.   [3] p. 79.   [4] p. 78.   [5] p. 92.

tion into an enormous activity; it has added the function of
research; and it has abandoned almost entirely the teaching or
transmission of culture.[1]

Four years later there was published the most thorough and
systematic examination of university problems that had appeared
in Britain since Cardinal Newman's discourses on *The Idea of a
University*. This was *The Crisis in the University*.[2] It was written
by Sir Walter Moberly, shortly before his retirement from the
post of Chairman of the University Grants Committee, which he
had held for thirteen years; but it incorporated with his thought
the results of prolonged discussions by a group of university
teachers and other people keenly interested in university problems, primarily from a Christian point of view.

The basic criticism of the contemporary universities made in
this book was the same as Gasset's: that they were 'not now dis-
charging their former cultural task'. This task was defined, in the
words of Professor Bonamy Dobrée, then Professor of English
Literature at Leeds University, as:[3]

... the creation, generation by generation in a continuous flow,
of a body of men and women who share a sense of civilised
values, who feel responsible for developing them, who are
united by their culture, and who by the simple pressure of
their existence and outlook will form and be enlightened public
opinion.

Moberly maintained that: 'most students go through our universities without ever having been forced to exercise their minds on
the issues which are really momentous'.[4] The universities,
instead of adhering to their traditional function of giving a broad
general education and inculcating in students a 'liberal and dis-
interested' attitude to study, were, whilst paying lip service to

[1] p. 57.
[2] Published for the Christian Frontier Council by the S.C.M.
Press, 1949.
[3] In an article in the *Political Quarterly*.
[4] Op. cit., p. 51.

these ideals, in fact turning out narrow specialists whose outlook was 'self-centred and utilitarian'.

The fundamental cause of this abnegation of their responsibility by the universities was, declared Moberly, a lack of 'any clear, agreed sense of direction and purpose'. In this the universities reflected 'the crisis in the world, and its pervading insecurity'. Because of this lack, of which they were well aware, the universities were increasingly unwilling to adopt any positive attitude towards ultimate questions; and therefore, said Moberly despairingly, had in their present state nothing creative to contribute to the world. Until they shook off their pose of academic neutrality they could not hope to give to the world that leadership which it was their traditional duty to give.

Space does not permit analysis of Moberly's view of the function of professing Christians as a 'creative minority' in the university, interesting though this is, nor a summary of that part of his book in which he ranges over the entire field of university life and work. But space must be found to record the six principles upon which he thought the university of today should build its corporate life.[1]

(i) the conviction that the things of the mind are worth pursuing, developed to an intensity at which it becomes an intellectual passion.

(ii) the duty of intellectual thoroughness, of pursuing the argument wherever it may lead.

(iii) the obligation to be meticulously accurate in dealing with empirical evidence.

(iv) the obligation to approach controversial questions with the temper of the judge rather than of the advocate or the notorious 'expert witness'.

(v) insistence on freedom of thought and publication.

(vi) the conviction that the university has indeed a social responsibility, but that this is first and foremost a responsibility for focussing the community's intellectual conscience.

[1] See pp. 121–126.

The book provoked widespread discussion. On the whole, informed opinion appeared to be generally on Moberly's side, though with many reservations about particular issues. There was, however, a body of root and branch opposition, led by Mr (now Professor) Michael Oakeshott, who roundly declared Moberly's proposed reforms to be both unnecessary and undesirable. Perhaps the most useful outcome of the prolonged controversy which followed the publication of the book was the fundamental thinking it provoked about the idea and functions of a university in the technological age of today and tomorrow.

The Autumn 1949 number of the *Universities Quarterly*, which consisted of a symposium of eight articles on 'The Mission of a University', showed how wide apart were individual views about these matters. On the one hand Professor M. L. Oliphant, then Professor of Physics at Birmingham University, declared his adherence to the traditional view that a university is 'a corporate body of individuals whose aim is to preserve and continually review knowledge and culture gained in the past, and aggressively to attack and extend the frontiers of knowledge'. Professor Oliphant felt that the British universities, including Oxford and Cambridge, had largely abandoned this conception, 'in favour of purely vocational training and investigations designed to solve *ad hoc* problems of the day, rather than to extend knowledge and scholarship'. He deplored this trend, and stated his conviction that 'the applied sciences, as at present taught and developed, are out of place in a university'.

Mr. John Adams, then Warden of Crewe Hall of Residence, Sheffield University, pleaded a diametrically opposite view with equal force and sincerity. Pointing out that 'from earliest times training for professional skills had been a characteristic function of the universities', he went on to ask:

Who is to say that the scientific study of materials, construction techniques, or forms of propulsion is not an important and worthy part of our culture? Is it not the duty of the university to promote such work and to provide facilities for undergraduates to enter upon it, provided that the social importance of the technology be established and that the discipline is such that the undergraduate is not given a mere technical drill, but is stimulated to think and inquire on logical scientific lines and to see the wider bearings of his study?

The U.G.C. have always striven to reconcile these conflicting points of view. Two quotations, from their reports on *University Development* in 1947–52 and 1935–47 respectively, illustrate their consistent attitude.

The essential functions of universities may be regarded as falling into two groups. One is to undertake original work . . . the second . . . the teaching of each new generation.[1]

No university of the future can escape the duty of furnishing the majority of its students with a type of training to some extent specifically related to their future careers. At the same time a university would in our view fail of its essential purpose if it did not, by some means or another, contrive to combine its vocational functions with the provision of a broad humanistic culture and a suitably tough intellectual discipline.[2]

But no one would say that either of these problems is yet resolved.

The object of this Part has been to examine critically some of the more important aspects of the present very large expansion of university education in England and Wales. It has not been to write a history of it. Consequently, many matters of great interest have not even been mentioned, and others have received but cursory treatment. Some at least of these will be discussed in Part III, where an attempt will be made to peer into the future from the background of the past and the present.

[1] Op. cit., p. 12.   [2] Op. cit., p. 60.

PART III

Future

CHAPTER ONE

The old . . . definition is straightforward: 'A university is a community of scholars who must guard, expand, and perpetuate knowledge.'
But now that time-honoured concept of the university begins to wear thin even in the Western world in which it originated and prospered.[1]

We may define a University, in British theory and practice, as an organised and degree-giving institution, intended for the study and advancement of the higher branches of learning, self-governing in its nature, and, to a greater or less extent, national in its scope. – ERNEST BARKER.[2]

The problems facing the British universities today are multifarious. They can, however, be divided broadly into two groups: those concerning internal administration and the conduct of university activities, and those posed by the ethos, intentions, and organisation of society. Most of the problems in the first group can, to some extent at any rate, be solved by the sole action of the universities themselves. None of those in the second group can.

The fundamental problem, which underlies, and determines the character of, all the others, is: What kind of institution is the university of tomorrow going to be? By this I do not mean what size it will be, what subjects it will teach, what students admit, what academic standards exact, or how it will be governed, financed, and administered. These are all highly important matters, which I shall in due course discuss, but they are all subsidiary to the basic question of what the essential nature of the

[1] *The Year Book of Education* 1959. Evans Bros., in association with the University of London Institute of Education and Teachers College, Columbia University, New York, 1959. Introduction by the joint Editors, George Z. F. Bereday and Joseph A. Lauwerys, pp. 1 and 2.
[2] *Universities in Great Britain*, S.C.M. Press, 1931, p. 9.

university will be, and consequently, since the two are inseparable, what its primary purpose will be.

The men of the Middle Ages, so we are led to believe, had no doubt whatever about either the nature or the purpose of a university. To them a university was, above all, a community: a community of scholars, of all ages and at all stages of maturity in learning, which had come together and cohered for the express purpose of preserving, advancing, and disseminating knowledge. As Sir Charles Grant Robertson has finely said:[1]

> If they were inspired by one passionate conviction, it was that membership in a university was *membership in a society*, that a course of university study is not merely the process of acquiring knowledge, but a life, that praying together and playing together are as important as working together, that examinations are tests of character as well as of capacity, and that a degree is a solemn admission to the full brotherhood of your fellow guildsmen.

Has that conviction grown cold? Is the idea of a university as first and foremost a community dying, or already dead, today? The Editors of *The Year Book of Education* 1959 would certainly appear to believe that it is on the way out, and as certainly Sir Ernest Barker's definition of a British university – written thirty years ago – contains no hint of it.

If we are in fact (whatever we may say) turning our backs upon the medieval concept of a university as a community, what essential features of the centuries-old idea of a university will the university of tomorrow retain? Among others, its social purpose, some people will reply, as does Sir Eric Ashby in his book *Technology and the Academics*.[2] Admitting that 'there are, of course, profound differences between those turbulent societies of students in fourteenth century Bologna and Paris and the prim Redbrick of the 1950s', Sir Eric nevertheless claims that 'the similarities are even more profound'.

'What has survived and is significant,' declares Sir Eric, 'is the social purpose of the university, its independence from Church

[1] In *The British Universities*, Methuen, 1944, p. 9.
[2] Macmillan, 1958, p. 2.

and State, and its peculiar method of internal government.'
Leaving aside for the moment the second and third of those three
items, may I say at once that I agree with Sir Eric that the social
purpose of the European university has, within broad limits,
remained constant throughout the ages? I would define that
purpose, briefly, as: to be society's principal means for conserving,
disseminating, and advancing academic knowledge; and, consequently, its principal source of supply of persons highly trained
in academic disciplines. But I believe the time to be fast approaching, if not already at hand, when in Britain there must be recon-
sideration of the nature and scope of that purpose and some
re-alignment of its elements.

I think there can be no doubt that the scholars of the Middle
Ages, had the question been pressed upon them, would have
declared with united voice that the pre-eminent function of the
university was to *advance* knowledge. There were other places in
which knowledge could be, and was being, conserved and dis-
seminated; but the university, while performing these functions,
was unique in that the creation of new knowledge was not only an
integral part of its purpose but the ultimate aim of all its academic
activities. There were, it is true – there always have been – individual scholars and groups of scholars committed to the same attitude and aim; but there was only one institution, the university,
which accepted the commitment as a corporate responsibility.

Today the situation is very different. The advancement of
knowledge has long ceased to be the monopoly, even among
corporate bodies, of the university. There are many institutions
devoted solely to original research. There are, too, many non-
university institutions taking up the three-fold task of conserving,
disseminating, and advancing knowledge which the university
had, over the centuries, made peculiarly its own. In England
and Wales the Advanced and Regional Colleges of Technology
are undertaking more and more research. There seems every
likelihood that before long they will become as fully committed
to it as are the universities, and, like them, will consider its
pursuit as essential for the quality and vigour of their teaching
and other academic activities. Nor are the technological colleges

the only non-university institutions developing this trend.

This is not to suggest for one moment that in the future the universities should do less research; indeed, with the ocean of knowledge ever broadening and deepening, they will inevitably have to do more. But it is to suggest that if original research, of all kinds, is to be prosecuted in our country systematically, efficiently, and economically, there must be far more co-operation and co-ordination than at present exists between the various institutions engaged upon it. And, while the inalienable right of every individual to pursue, in his own time, whatever research he desires must at all costs be safeguarded, increased co-operation and co-ordination between institutions may necessitate the allocation to each of broad areas which will be regarded as their special responsibility. The rapidly growing amount of contract research work being done by the universities and the colleges of technology for the government and industry seems to point to the necessity to explore this matter – and may indeed point to the answer.

Research in universities cannot be divorced from teaching. Nor can it today in any institution of advanced education. The situation has changed in respect of teaching as well as of research; and it will change still more in the days to come. Until recently the universities were virtually the only bodies engaged in teaching at the highest levels. That is no longer the case. Students in the Colleges of Advanced Technology and the Regional Colleges of Technology may now pursue courses of study leading to the Diploma in Technology (Dip. Tech.) and beyond that to the Membership of the College of Technologists (M.C.T.), awards which are officially rated as comparable in standards with the university degrees of Bachelor with Honours and Ph.D. And there is no reason to believe that these will be the only high-level courses and high-ranking awards that will be created for students in institutions other than universities.

What will be the essential differences between such courses and university courses? Will they be procedural only – for example, the university undergraduate remaining a wholly full-time student, while the Dip. Tech. student, as at present, follows a 'sandwich' course of alternate full-time periods in college and at the works?

Or will the differences penetrate deeply into the content of the courses and the methods of teaching? In the latter case – and it seems almost inevitable that this will happen – the criteria for the selection of students for the various forms of higher education will have to be radically reconsidered. Otherwise, one of two entirely deplorable situations will obtain. Either there will be perpetual body-snatching by the universities and the other institutions, each striving to secure the ablest minds, or, as seems at present more likely, the universities will continue to skim off most of the richest intellectual cream and leave to the other institutions only the second and lower grades.

Original research, and teaching at the highest levels will, it seems certain, be in the future increasingly shared between universities and other types of institution. What, then, will a university have to offer that is unique? One is driven back to the idea of community. Outdated though this idea may seem to some people to be, it may well provide the answer. Not in precisely the same terms, perhaps, as did the medieval idea, but maybe in terms more nearly fitted to the circumstances of today and tomorrow: in terms of an environment which affords – indeed, compels – a particular kind of academic and social experience. All the non-university institutions will presumably be more or less specialised – if any should extend their range of subjects over several fields of knowledge it would be difficult to deny them the title of university. This wide range would be a unique characteristic of a university. But, clearly, great range without cohesion would not make a community; its unrestrained effect would, in fact, be the opposite, to break up the whole into self-contained and largely isolated parts: and there is reason to fear that this is actually happening in some of our universities. It may well happen in many more if the present tendency to keep on increasing student numbers in existing universities continues.

What, then, are the conditions necessary to facilitate a sense of community? And, since this Part is not an essay in Utopia-building, but an attempt to examine possible lines of future university development in our country, what are the chances that such conditions will be considered, deemed essential, and satisfied?

CHAPTER TWO

The first question to be decided is whether there exists an optimum size for a university – GRAEME C. MOODIE.[1]

If the university of the future is to be no more than one among several types of institution providing higher education and doing original research, its size will not greatly matter. It can be determined by purely material considerations: the site available, the number of Faculties and Departments, the size of the demand for graduates in the subjects it teaches, and so on. But if a university is to be a community, then clearly there must be some limit to both its total size and the size of its constituent parts; and its buildings and other facilities must be reasonably concentrated. To what extent does the present situation admit of the possibility of such conditions being satisfied?

Despite the post-war expansion most British universities are, by comparison with those of many other countries, relatively small; at the beginning of the academic year 1959–60 only London had a student population of over 10,000, and most of the universities, as will be seen from the table on the opposite page, had fewer than half that number.

It will be seen that of the twenty-one universities listed only eight had in October 1959 student populations exceeding 5,000. Of these, all but one consist of two or more establishments. London includes over thirty colleges, schools, and institutes. Oxford and Cambridge are collegiate universities. The University of Wales is a federation of four colleges and a medical school. Durham consists of two Divisions, one at Durham and the other at Newcastle-upon-Tyne. Glasgow and Manchester have affiliated

[1] *The Universities: a Royal Commission?* The Fabian Society, 1959, p. 25.

FULL-TIME UNIVERSITY STUDENTS,
October, 1959[1]

ENGLAND

London	21,509
Cambridge	8,938
Oxford	8,807
Manchester, including the Manchester College of Science and Technology	6,000
Durham – Durham Colleges 1,463 King's College, Newcastle 3,621	5,084
Leeds	4,655
Birmingham	4,112
Liverpool	3,770
Bristol	3,227
Sheffield	2,817
Nottingham	2,456
Hull	1,581
Reading	1,555
Southampton	1,551
Exeter	1,280
Leicester	1,201
University College of North Staffordshire	732

WALES

University College of Cardiff	1,926
University College of Aberystwyth	1,480
University College of Swansea	1,358
University College of Bangor	1,191
National School of Medicine	150
	6,105

[1] Figures kindly supplied by the U.G.C. before publication.

SCOTLAND

Glasgow, including the Royal College of Science and Technology	7,074
Edinburgh	5,404
St. Andrews, including Queen's College, Dundee	2,459
Aberdeen	1,882

to them large colleges of science and technology. Only Edinburgh is a unitary university.

At the other end of the scale, nine of the universities, and the University College of North Staffordshire, had fewer than 3,000 students; and of these ten institutions seven had fewer than 2,000. To this group should be added also the four colleges in the University of Wales, because for geographical reasons they must always remain more or less separate and self-contained bodies. By the same token, one could similarly include the Durham Division of the University of Durham.

If one were to accept, quite arbitrarily, and purely for the sake of the argument,[1] the figure of 3,000 as being the maximum number for a unitary university institution in which it is possible for members spending a minimum of three years in it to meet and mix and share activities, intellectual, social, and recreative, to such an extent as to feel a strong and genuine sense of common interest, then, on the basis of the 1959 figures well over half of the British universities and university colleges would fall within the category in which this sense of community would be possible. Of the ten which are above the limit Oxford and Cambridge can be left out of consideration, for their colleges are communities of the highest order. London is, of course, in its existing form, quite hopeless. The late Dr Abraham Flexner's acid comment upon it, made [2] thirty years ago, is just as applicable today:

[1] This is not to say that I do accept it; I do not know the appropriate number.

[2] In *Universities: American, English, German*, Oxford University Press, 1930, pp. 231-2.

If a university is, whatever its type or form, a highly vitalised organism, vitalised, not by administrative means, but by ideas and ideals, with a corporate life, I confess myself unable to understand in what sense the University of London is a university at all . . . it is a line drawn about an enormous number of different institutions of heterogeneous quality and purpose.

In my opinion, the only cure for London would be its division into the five universities which already exist in all but name within it: University College in the north, King's College in the south, the Imperial College of Science and Technology in the west, Queen Mary College in the east, and the post-graduate university in and around the Senate House in the centre. But though this idea has occurred to other minds than mine there is, so far as I know, little reason for hoping that it will be realised in the near future.

Among the unitary universities there were in 1959 only five above the 3,000 mark: Birmingham, Bristol, Edinburgh, Leeds, and Liverpool. Of these, unfortunately, three – Bristol, Edinburgh and Liverpool – are located in the centre of large cities on sites which seem to compel piecemeal expansion. The smaller universities are as a group far more happily placed: Exeter, Hull, Nottingham, Reading, and the University Colleges of Swansea and North Staffordshire are all on estates which allow both concentration of premises and ready access to open spaces; and Aberdeen, Aberystwyth, Cardiff, and Leicester all possess something of the same advantage.

But my analysis thus far has been based on the student population figures for October 1959. As everyone knows, those figures are already surpassed, and will be much more so. Practically all the universities and colleges are scheduled to expand largely in the course of the 1960s. In January 1959 *The Times Educational Supplement* wrote that:

> If the U.G.C.'s plans go through unchanged the proportion of students, excluding London, Cambridge, and Oxford, in universities of fewer than 3,000 would be reduced from more than half three years ago to a third in the late 1960s.[1]

[1] *The Times Educational Supplement*, January 14th, 1959.

That was on the basis of the plans for expansion agreed at that time between the universities and the Government: that is, a total of 124,000 university students in Great Britain in the mid-1960s, and possibly something like 136,000 by 1970. But early in 1960 the Government asked the U.G.C. to discuss with the universities the possibility of increasing the total number of student places in Great Britain to 170,000 or 175,000 by, at latest, the early 1970s. The result of these discussions had not, at the time of writing, been disclosed, but the indications were that most universities were prepared to make their due contribution; indeed, they were described by a Government spokesman[1] as 'in a mood for expansion', and one at least offered more than the U.G.C. suggested. Several of the larger universities, however, including London, Oxford and Cambridge, were by no means eager to expand, at any rate in proportion to their existing numbers, and the A.U.T. declared itself strongly opposed to any attempt to provide the 170,000–175,000 places within the existing universities.

We believe that there should be a deliberate policy of preserving the pattern of university life found in the smaller and medium sized universities.[2]

With that opinion I entirely agree; and the fact that it has been publicly expressed by an influential body of university teachers encourages me to hope that a halt may be called to a seemingly endless process of blowing up the size of our universities – seemingly endless, because there is no reason to believe 175,000 to be to be the final target. I admit that, with the 1960–3 university building programme so far advanced as it is, the hope seems at present slight. (The buildings could, of course, be used to give fewer students more room, a not undesirable prospect.) There are, I think, three measures which could be taken to prevent our universities from swelling to inordinate size: the creation of new universities and university colleges, including, in the latter category, some 'junior' colleges, the diversion of considerable numbers of students who would otherwise enter universities into

[1] See *The Times*, May 12th, 1960.
[2] *The Times Educational Supplement*, May 27th, 1960.

FUTURE   129

colleges of technology, and the shedding by the universities of some subjects now in their programmes.

In 1958 Professor W. G. V. Balchin, professor of Geography at Swansea, produced a most interesting report, based on a study of the distribution of population in England and Wales, in which he proposed the establishment of fourteen additional university institutions, to be set up at:

Brighton	Lincoln
Canterbury	Norwich
Carlisle	Plymouth
Cheltenham with	Shrewsbury
Gloucester	Truro
Hereford	Weymouth
Ipswich	York
Lancaster	

Professor Balchin's argument,[1] briefly, was that universities are a product of population, and arise in response to national, civic, or regional needs. National universities tended to appear first, and then civic universities related to large urban populations. The national and civic forces which had produced the pattern of universities existing in 1958 were by then largely satisfied. But – and this was the core of his argument – as the standard of living rose, so the size of the population needed to support a university diminished. The time was at hand when regions might be expected to produce university institutions. Their needs should be met, because the direct influence of a university upon its neighbourhood did not appear to extend beyond a radius of about twenty miles. If the existing pattern of universities were maintained the results would be very large universities in the large conurbations, and very large tracts of country unprovided with university facilities. His scheme would produce an even distribution over the whole country.

Of the centres in Professor Balchin's list Brighton had already

[1] *A Geographical Conspectus*, by Professor W. G. V. Balchin, University College of Swansea. Privately distributed.

been encouraged by the U.G.C. to go ahead with its plans for a University of Sussex. In April 1960 proposals submitted by Norwich and York were approved in principle by the U.G.C. At the time of writing formal applications were being considered by the Committee from Gloucester and Cheltenham, Warwickshire, Essex, and Kent. Tentative discussions had also been held in other places, including the new town of Stevenage.

I do not wish to make too much of this measure, because I think that for three reasons it would be unlikely to make a very large contribution during the coming decade. First, not all of the proposals may mature; evidence of substantial local support is required before the U.G.C. will consider approval. Secondly, a long time elapses between the approval of proposals and the opening of a college – in the case of North Staffordshire it was five years, and it looks as if Brighton will be not much speedier.[1] Thirdly, if North Staffordshire is a reliable precedent, a new college starts in a very small way and builds up its strength only slowly. North Staffordshire opened with 150 students, and after nine years had grown only to 730.

Along with the creation of new universities and colleges could well go the partition of one or two existing universities. London, the prime example, has already been referred to. Durham and Newcastle appear to have agreed to separate, and moves are on foot to make the four constituent colleges of the University of Wales into universities; I hope these will be successful, and that ultimately Lampeter, at last on the U.G.C. grant list, will become a university. Perhaps, too, Dundee might be Scotland's fifth university. Such partitions would allow for expansion without inflation, and (except in London) more fully satisfy the regional needs which Professor Balchin so rightly argues should be satisfied.

The idea of the 'junior' college has been mooted in two forms: as an annexe to an existing university in which all, or most, of the

---

[1] Despite the fact that the date of starting work at the University of Sussex was in March 1960 advanced by two years, from October 1963 to October 1961. Even so, three and a half years will have elapsed between approval and opening.

first-year undergraduates would be taught, and as a separate and independent institution which, like the American Junior College, would offer only the earlier stages of the courses leading to first degrees. The first of these forms seems to me to have more disadvantages than advantages, but the second could, I think, make a very valuable contribution, by no means limited to easing the pressure of numbers on the universities. It could enrol the 'borderliners' about whose potential the university felt doubt and other students who on leaving school are just short of the required qualifications for university entry. Many, perhaps most, of its students would clearly have reached their ceiling by the end of, say, a two-year course, but some undoubtedly will mature beyond expectation; these could, if they so desired, apply for entry into the university, with exemption from part of the first degree course. The Secondary Modern school has shown, at a lower level, that given a more leisurely course children of apparently lesser intellectual potential can reach Grammar school levels; the same could confidently be expected to happen in the 'junior' college.

The immediate result of the second measure I propose – the diversion of applicants from universities to colleges of technology – is highly speculative. Some who were diverted might refuse to accept the option, and the colleges of technology might not have places for others. But the increasing number of Grammar school pupils entering colleges of technology to prepare for the Dip. Tech. (small though the total number is as yet) suggests that such diversion might not be so unpopular as many people might fear. In any case, I regard it as an absolute necessity, in the interests of both the nation and of individual students.

So far as I know, no forecasts of university student numbers have taken into consideration the possibility of a sizeable proportion of young people qualified by ability and attainments to enter universities going instead into colleges of technology. The U.G.C.'s figures appear to be based solely on considerations of available accommodation and staffing, those of the A.U.T. and other bodies on estimates of the numbers of young people who will have the requisite ability for university studies. Were it accepted in practice, as it is in theory, that colleges of technology preparing students for the Dip. Tech. should recruit from the same intellectual levels as the universities the estimates of future university students might be considerably reduced – and numerous able young people would get more appropriate courses. There are already ten Colleges of Advanced Technology and some twenty-five Regional Colleges – together more than the number of universities and university colleges – and there is no *a priori* reason why the number of colleges in each group should not be considerably increased. (It is intended, I understand, to raise the number of Regional Colleges to between thirty and forty.) Their available accommodation for students doing degree-equivalent studies is not at present large, for they have many other courses to carry; but it could be increased.

My third measure would, of course, be highly unpopular, because the prestige of belonging to the university is, very rightly, highly prized, and would not willingly be relinquished, however much the facilities and conditions of service in other institutions were improved and the intellectual calibre of the students raised. But sooner or later, if intolerable congestion in the university programmes is to be avoided, and university work restricted to the academic disciplines which are its proper concern, the question must be faced whether purely professional studies should any longer figure in university programmes, and if so, on what grounds, and to what extent.

Professional studies have been connected with university education from the start, when three professions, law, medicine, and the Church, played a large part in bringing it into being. Those professions are connected with it still, but in England on very different footings. Medicine is a full and prominent member, though the professional part of medical studies is carried out in teaching hospitals, that is, in establishments affiliated to universities but primarily devoted to non-educational purposes. Professional law studies are conducted outside the university, in establishments not affiliated to it, though law is studied in all the universities, and the degrees awarded are valuable entrance qualifications for the higher reaches of the profession. The university teaches theology, but does not train ministers of religion, Teaching, which originated inside the Church, is one part in the university and three parts outside it, though the training colleges are now linked academically (but not organically) with the universities through the Institutes of Education.

Engineering was introduced in the nineteenth century by the modern universities. Since then the widest variety of technologies, ranging from brewing at Birmingham to glass technology at Sheffield and textiles at Leeds and Manchester, has been added. Similar incursions have taken place in other fields; quite unsystematically, as the following brief analysis will show. Accountancy figures in the programme of seventeen universities but banking in only four and commerce in only seven. Architecture is taught at nine universities, but building, today one of the nation's largest industries, at only three, while that most important modern profession, town and country planning, which has close links with a dozen university disciplines, from geography and geology through mathematics to sociology, has as yet found a place in only two – the same number as estate management. Agriculture has secured a firm footing, for it is taught in twelve universities, but its sister craft, horticulture, figures in only three, though forestry is found in five.

Similar anomalies exist on what has come to be called the 'Arts' side of the university – somewhat of a misnomer, for the Fine Arts can be studied at only five universities, though four others offer courses in the history of art. Music is taught in all the British universities, but Drama in only one. Among modern languages Portuguese occupies as many places as Russian.

Even if no subjects were dropped from the university programme, this could be greatly lightened, and its purpose much clarified, if all purely professional studies and activities were transferred to other institutions – associated, perhaps, with the universities, after the fashion of the teaching hospitals or the teacher training colleges – and the universities were left only with the task of teaching the academic disciplines which are the bases of these professional activities. That, after all, was the criterion on which some, at least, of them were admitted:

The Basic Idea in the creation of the Faculty of Commerce in the University of Birmingham . . . was not that a university could provide trained business men . . . but that it could provide those whose profession was to be 'industry' or 'business' with a three years' discipline in the fundamentals of the problems that they would meet in their professional careers.[1]

Could that be said of all the first degree courses now being given in British universities?

Lest I should be accused of presumptuously (or even maliciously) thinking up a proposal from which all rightminded men must recoil, may I say that it has a highly respectable ancestry? To give but two pieces of evidence, in June 1909 the Lords of the Treasury stated[2] that they agreed with the Advisory Committee on Grants to University Colleges that:

State aid to general education of a University standard should, as far as possible, be distinguished from State aid to professional and technical education.

Twenty years later Abraham Flexner said[3] bluntly that:

A university abdicates its function if it undertakes a course in the salesmanship of coal; it is within its sphere in dealing with the sciences involved in mining – physics, chemistry, and metallurgy.

To conclude this chapter, may I explain why I hope to see our universities kept small enough to enable them to be communities as well as centres of higher learning? I think I can best do so in words written by Cardinal Newman and Sir Richard Livingstone. Newman said:[4]

[1] Sir Charles Grant Robertson, op. cit., p. 64.
[2] Treasury Minute dated June 3rd, 1909.
[3] Flexner, op. cit., p. 256.
[4] *The Scope and Nature of University Education*. Discourse 7. Quoted from *Newman on University Education*, edited by Roger J. McHugh, Browne & Nolan, 1944, p. 72.

If then a practical end must be assigned to a University course, I say it is that of training good members of society. Its art is the art of social life, and its end is fitness for the world.

And that training is of supreme importance because, as Livingstone says:[1]

The education which [the universities] give moulds the outlook of all educated men, and thus affects politics, administration, the professions, industry and commerce. Their discoveries and their thought penetrate almost every activity of life.

But, of course, smallness of size does not in itself make an institution into a community. Other favourable conditions must also be present. I turn to what I consider the most important of all these: residence.

[1] *The Rainbow Bridge*, Pall Mall Press, 1959, pp. 12–13.

CHAPTER THREE

I've got to know the city of X pretty thoroughly since I've been here . . .
I only wish I'd been able to get to know the university half as well.[1]

The quality of a university student's private life is of fundamental importance; it can make or mar his university career. To my mind, and here I speak from personal experience – though not, unfortunately, as a student – there is no adequate substitute for the community life of a college or hall of residence. That opinion I share with a very great many other university people.

As has been recorded in Part I, centuries ago Oxford and Cambridge began to abandon the practice of residence in lodgings, and even in licensed and supervised hostels, in favour of collegiate residence. The result was a marked improvement in intellectual, social, and disciplinary standards. The progenitors of the modern universities, being essentially local colleges, naturally assumed that their students would live at home. As the geographical range of these colleges widened, the equally natural assumption was made that students from outlying districts would, if daily journeys proved too laborious and time-consuming for them, find themselves lodgings. Here and there, it is true, enlightened benefactors were moved to provide small hostels, usually for specialised groups of students, but in general the provision of living accommodation for students was considered to be outside the province of the colleges; and this attitude persisted to some extent after their elevation into universities. As the U.G.C. wrote in their first Report:

---

[1] A university student, on going down after four years. Quoted by Professor W. R. Niblett, article in *The Times Educational Supplement*, December 12th, 1958.

Much was already being done before 1914 to promote a corporate University life, but at the stage of development then reached by most of the Institutions [i.e., on the U.G.C. grant list] provision for social needs was inevitably regarded as of secondary importance.[1]

The Committee set themselves at once to correct this attitude. 'Such provision,' they went on to say, 'has now become an immediate and urgent duty.' And from that moment the U.G.C. have never ceased to campaign for increased provision of halls of residence, 'expressly built for that purpose', which even then they regarded as the only 'permanently satisfactory solution' of student living at the university. In their last quinquennial Report before the 1939-45 war[2] they explained in detail why they held this conviction.

As compared with lodgings or with many homes, a hall affords an environment where intellectual interests are strong. It offers students exceptionally favourable opportunities for the stimulating interplay of mind with mind, for the formation of friendships, and for learning the art of understanding and living with others of outlook and temperament unlike their own. It can be, and it often is, a great humanising force. Moreover, in Universities where so many students disperse immediately after the working day is done, the halls, as continuous centres of corporate life, do something to stimulate that life in the University as a whole.

Up to that time, despite the fact that on their visitations they encountered almost everywhere 'the desire that there should be more accommodation in suitable residential halls', they had had only very limited success, owing largely to the fact that they had been unable to make more than microscopic contributions from Treasury funds towards the building of halls. As they sadly recorded in 1930:

[1] Report of the University Grants Committee, 1921, p. 14.
[2] *University Development from 1929-30 to 1934-5*, University Grants Committee, H.M.S.O., 1936, p. 17.

We have ourselves done what the means at our disposal allowed, to help Universities and Colleges in their attempts to meet the increasing demand for places in residential halls, but this has inevitably gone but a small way to solve what is an extensive problem . . .[1]

Scrutiny of the universities' annual accounts from 1921 to 1928, as presented in the U.G.C. Returns, suggests that the average amount available to the U.G.C. for 'Grants to subsidiary Accounts (Hostels, etc.)' was not much more than one-tenth of one per cent of the total university expenditure. It is not surprising that in their 1928–9 Report the U.G.C. had once again to throw the ball back to 'private donors'. Not altogether unsuccessfully; by 1937–8 the proportion of students in halls (outside Oxford and Cambridge) had risen from 15 to 20 per cent. But nearly one-sixth of all the students in hostels were at two of the youngest and smallest university institutions: Reading University and the University College of the South West at Exeter. At both of these well over 70 per cent of the students were in residence.

After the second world war the U.G.C. renewed their campaign, despite the fact that a Commission of Enquiry[2] set up by the Committee of Vice-Chancellors and Principals reported in 1948 that the capital cost of providing desirable halls of residence appeared to be about £1,500 to £1,800 a student place, or something like £250,000 for a hall of 150 students. To provide sufficient residential accommodation to enable the whole of a student population of 88,000 (as it then was) to participate would cost not less than £50,000,000. Even to accommodate as high a proportion (25·1 per cent) as in 1939 would demand an expenditure of about £8,000,000.

Nevertheless, in the same report[3] in which they recorded the findings of the Murray Commission the U.G.C. declared that they

[1] U.G.C. report for the year 1928–9, H.M.S.O., 1930, p. 42.

[2] Chairman, Sir Keith Murray, then Rector of Lincoln College, Oxford.

[3] *University Development from 1935 to 1947*, University Grants Committee, H.M.S.O., 1948, see pp. 54 and 55.

remained 'warmly in favour of the policy of immensely increasing residential accommodation at the earliest possible moment', and drew particular attention to 'the fact that halls of residence are much more than a means of providing living accommodation for students'. In their next quinquennial report[1] they recorded as 'one of the outstanding disappointments of the past quinquennium' the fact that 'so little has been possible to increase the proportion of students enjoying the benefits of residence in halls of residence'. This despite the fact that by 1951–2 the number of such students in the universities of England and Wales (Oxford and Cambridge excepted) had risen above the 1938–9 level – owing largely to grants made by the U.G.C., which had assisted more than a dozen projects during the quinquennium. The U.G.C. admitted regretfully that they saw 'little prospect of any immediate expansion of the residential system', but made clear that they would say nothing that would 'discourage universities from thinking ahead to a period in which conditions will permit the resumption of building on a larger scale'.

The figures produced by the Murray Commission had ·undoubtedly caused many people to think again about halls of residence, and probably nipped in the bud a number of intended projects. The increased proportion of students in residence in 1951–2 had been achieved largely, not by new building, but by the purchase and adaptation of existing premises, usually large private residences: an expedient not always entirely satisfactory, either from the point of view of accommodation or maintenance costs.

In January 1956 the U.G.C. appointed a sub-committee, under the chairmanship of Professor W. R. Niblett, then Director of the University of Leeds Institute of Education, to make an exhaustive investigation into the whole question of residential accommodation. The terms of reference given to this sub-committee were truly comprehensive:

To consider and report on the nature and importance of the role which should be played by halls of residence in the education

[1] *University Development from 1947 to 1952*, H.M.S.O., 1953, p. 28.

of university students, and its relationship to that of other forms of student organisation; the manner in which halls of residence should be administered and staffed in order to carry out this role; and the arrangements within universities for formulating policy on these matters and for supervising its execution.

The Sub-committee's Report,[1] published in 1957, was a masterly document which fully confirmed the U.G.C.'s belief that:

for most students there is no satisfactory substitute for a properly conducted hall of residence if they are to participate fully in the education of the student by the student which is one of the most important parts of a university education.[2]

Now, if this be true, as I am convinced it is, the question of Halls of Residence – not simply residential accommodation – is one of the most crucial issues of university policy which must be resolved. The country is spending annually very large, and constantly increasing, sums of money on university education for a high proportion of its ablest minds. If it can be shown that this education, in order to be made as adequate as possible, requires that most students attending non-collegiate universities shall spend at least some part of their university life in halls of residence, then it is false economy not to provide sufficient halls, large though the capital cost would undoubtedly be.

Both the U.G.C. and their Sub-committee appear completely convinced that the case for halls of residence has been fully made. The U.G.C.'s opinion has already been quoted. Their sub-committee, which enquired in detail about the desirable nature, size, government, amenities and educational benefits of halls of residence, and about possible alternatives, concluded[3] that 'halls of residence can, and should, play a highly important part in the general education of university students', and that 'in every case our witnesses were at pains to make clear that in educative value the alternative was a second best. We emphatically endorse this view'.[4]

---

[1] *Halls of Residence*, H.M.S.O., 1957.
[2] *University Development* 1952–7, H.M.S.O., 1958, p. 27.
[3] Op. cit., p. 16.   [4] p. 40.

In the case of both the U.G.C. and its sub-committee, it should be emphasised that their views reflect the opinion of a very large and varied body of people. It is only fair to add, however, that not everybody, even among those who work in universities, is entirely of this opinion. Some of these people, probably the great majority, believe that the provision of large blocks of study bedrooms, either with a cafeteria and common rooms in the same building, or in close proximity to the Students' Union, university refectory, library, laboratories, and other facilities and amenities, would meet the case equally, or almost equally, well. Plans for such buildings at Leeds and Manchester have been announced; and until these – to be followed, no doubt, by others – have been in operation for some years it would be foolish to hazard any judgment on such projects.

There is also a body of opinion, probably very small, which is not convinced that residence is essential. In its extreme form this view was expressed in a letter to *The Times Educational Supplement*[1] which spoke of the belief in the value of residence as an 'obsession', and of shutting young people up 'in little private worlds, insulating them most carefully from all contact with life'.

All I will say of that opinion is that, having visited many halls of residence, and lived in one for four-and-a-half years, I can find nothing in my experience to support it. On the contrary, I have become absolutely convinced that the student living in a well-managed and well-conducted hall of residence enjoys so many advantages over the student who lives in lodgings as to put his university career on an entirely different plane. He has every opportunity to enjoy 'the education of the student by the student', for in a hall of residence of any size will be found representatives of every Faculty and most departments in the university, and of every year of student life, undergraduate and post-graduate. He has, if he so desires, excellent opportunities to learn the practice of democracy through active participation in Junior Common Room management. On the other hand, if he wants to devote himself uninterruptedly to his academic studies he has a comfortable,

[1] March 6th, 1959.

well appointed bed-sitting room specifically designed and equipped for the purpose. Yet he will not be thereby insulated from contact with his fellows, for he must meet them each day at meals if at no other times. Everything is 'laid on' for him; meals are at fixed times (and punctual), rooms are cleaned regularly, games, reading and common rooms are available. Tenure is certain. The hall is usually (though not invariably) within easy range of the university's teaching accommodation. Finally, and most importantly, in a hall of residence a student has continuously at his service at least one adult of standing and experience, the Warden, to whom he can at any time take any personal problems which are distressing him. Frequently he has other adults also, for in many halls members of the university academic staff are resident. At the least this provides opportunities for social contacts between staff and students; at best, as has happened in some halls, it can develop into something approaching the tutorial system in the Oxford and Cambridge colleges.

I have enumerated the advantages only of life in a hall of residence. I am well aware that there can be disadvantages and defects. A hall may be badly managed. Rules may be too restrictive, or the government too paternal – or maternal. There may be friction between the Senior and the Junior Common Rooms, or between individual students and staff. Cliques may form, petty forms of persecution occur, and shy or unpopular students made to feel more lonely than in lodgings. The food may be indifferent or institutional, the public rooms poorly furnished and decorated. All this can be remedied by initiative and imagination.

To say in general terms that residence in hall insulates a student from 'all contact with life' seems to me meaningless. From what 'life'? Certainly not from the academic life of the university, participation in which is, after all, the purpose for which the student has come to the university. This, as I have tried to show, it greatly facilitates. The charge is sometimes made that the social activities available in hall tend to withdraw students from the social activities provided by the Students' Union for the university at large. This may happen, as it does in all organisations where both general and sectional activities are being carried on side by side. But I doubt if it happens to any serious extent. I have information about one hall only; this shows that over a period of years its members have been very well represented in Union activities of all kinds. As for participation in cultural activities provided for the general public, my impression – again, based on experience in one hall only – is that hall members participate as fully as any young people of their age, and more so than most. And – if this be 'contact with life' – they do a great deal of paid employment during vacations.

It is frequently alleged that halls of residence limit a student's independence, and more frequently that they are too expensive for many students. I can find little justification for either complaint. Students who live at home (still nearly a quarter of all university students) all too frequently enjoy less independence than students in halls. 'For most students the worst place in which to live is their own home, which is often cramped, and in which they always have many obligations and distractions.'[1]

Lodgings may be comfortable and convenient; or they may not. At best, living in lodgings inevitably imposes upon a student some degree of isolation from the main stream of university life. At worst, it means living in lonely squalor. And, to quote Mr Campbell again: 'Greater prosperity, smaller homes, the restrictions imposed on council house tenants, and competition for all-the-year-round industrial and commercial lodgers means that the supply of suitable lodgings has failed to increase with the demand'.[2] At present, the demand increases constantly; both absolutely and relatively the number of students living in lodgings increases year by year. In 1951–2 the proportion was 39·6 per cent, in 1958–9 49·6 per cent.

The charge for residence in hall is, on the average, undoubtedly higher than that for lodgings; at Sheffield in 1960 the compara-

[1] P. W. Campbell, article in *Crossbow* (journal of the Conservative 'Bow Group'), Summer 1959, p. 53. But see also article by Miss Alice Eden, reporting on a survey of social life in provincial universities, in the *British Journal of Sociology*, December, 1959, pp. 291–310.

[2] Loc. cit.

tive figures were, approximately, £5 and £3 10s. 0d. a week. But when the cost of bus fares, often considerable, outside meals, and the various 'extras' – for heating and other incidentals – which may be charged in lodgings are taken into account, the difference may be not nearly so large as superficially it appears to be. And when the amenities of a hall are compared with those of most lodgings, there can be no doubt which, in terms of value received, is the cheaper.

The universities have planned to spend between 1958 and 1963 some £18,000,000 on building new halls and enlarging existing ones. That estimate was based upon a student population of 124,000 rising possibly to 136,000. On that basis the increased accommodation proposed would undoubtedly have improved matters considerably, though not to the extent that many people would have liked. With 170,000 students it would leave the situation rather worse than it is at present; there would be, I calculate, not quite so large a proportion of students in residence, and – to me the most terrifying feature – a very much larger number of students who would have to be accommodated in lodgings. In many university cities today it is difficult enough to secure even a sufficient number of lodgings, without too nice a regard for quality; how at least double the present number will be found – and that is what it will mean unless there is a very substantial increase in the number of halls of residence – passes the imagination.

CHAPTER FOUR

. . . the undergraduate, who, when all is said, is the real centre of everything in any University. – T. R. GLOVER.[1]

In December 1957 the Vice-Chancellor of Liverpool University described the system of selecting students for university education as one of 'fumbling uncertainties'. The following November he warned his University Court that the educational problem of the mid-1960s would be, not the eleven-plus examination for secondary school selection, but the 18-plus selection for university entry. In those two statements Sir James Mountford put moderately complaints about university selection which have driven many other people to far more violent language.

There are many causes for complaint: they may perhaps be summarised by saying that the procedures employed by the universities for selecting and rejecting applicants are chaotic and competitive, and that consequently, since there are more applicants than places:

> Boys and girls are hawking themselves, or are being hawked by their heads, round the universities and colleges. They aim not at admission to the most suitable course at the most appropriate university, but at finding room somewhere at all costs . . . It is probably true that some applicants do not deserve university education, but there is no doubt that already satisfactory students cannot get a place.[2]

Under 'procedures' I distinguish, (i) means used by universities, and within them by faculties and departments, to determine the eligibility of applicants for places, and (ii) the machinery used

[1] *Cambridge Retrospect*, p. 114.
[2] From a memorandum by the Chief Education Officer for Dorset, quoted in *Education*, August 23rd, 1957.

by universities to inform applicants of acceptance or rejection. An admirable exposé of (i) is made in the Report of the Central Advisory Council for Education – England (the 'Crowther' Report), 15 to 18;[1] it must suffice here to say that these means include special examinations (held at different times in the year), demands by faculties and departments for qualifying standards above that officially acceptable to the university, whether in the form of a larger number of subjects passed at 'A' level in the G.C.E., or higher percentage marks, or both, interviews, school records, and head teachers' confidential letters – to which some L.E.A.s add a further screening of applicants for grants. About attempts, not unsuccessful, to improve (ii) I shall say something in a moment.

It is not surprising that, faced with the jungle of (i), would-be entrants apply to many universities, thus making confusion worse confounded.

Such was, and still is, the confusion that no one knows how many 'already satisfactory students' fail to secure places, though a most exhaustive inquiry[2] made between 1955 and 1957 by Mr R. K. Kelsall, then lecturer at the London School of Economics, at the request of the Committee of Vice-Chancellors and Principals, threw considerable light upon the situation. But Mr Kelsall was fatally handicapped by the fact that no figures were available for admissions to Oxford and Cambridge, easily the most sought-after universities. He discovered that, exclusive of applications to those universities, there were in 1955 70,000 applications made by 31,000 candidates; that is to say, on average each candidate had applied to two or three universities; that when the academic year started 13,000 candidates had failed to get places – and that the universities had about 2,500 places unfilled. Of the disappointed candidates some had not the required academic qualifications; but of those who had about 2,500 (exclusive of overseas candidates) never obtained places.

[1] H.M.S.O., 1959. See pp. 290–4.
[2] *Report on an Inquiry into Applications for Admission to Universities*, by R. K. Kelsall, Association of Universities of the British Commonwealth, 1957.

In 1958 the Committee of Vice-Chancellors and Principals appointed a committee to investigate means used by universities for receiving applications and offering places. This committee, reporting in May 1958,[1] recommended more uniform application forms, and standard final dates for making applications and for acceptance or rejection of offers of places. These recommendations eased the situation somewhat, but did not touch the real problem, which is that in most cases the universities have not sufficient time in which to make properly considered selection.

The very large majority of applicants rely upon passes in the General Certificate of Education (at A level) to qualify them academically for university entry. Many have not got all the required passes when they apply. The main G.C.E. examinations are held in June-July, and the results are not published until August. The university year begins in early October. That is the situation in a nutshell. The universities can only give provisional acceptance to unqualified candidates, to be confirmed when the required passes have been obtained. Many candidates have received two, three or more provisional acceptances. Some have obtained the required G.C.E. passes by August, some have not; and the whole tangle has to be sorted out within a month.

There is only one solution to this problem, to put back the date of the G.C.E. examination. The date most frequently suggested is around Easter; my own preference is for the previous November, when G.C.E. examinations are already held. The objection raised to an earlier examination is that candidates will be so many months younger, and therefore less well prepared, and that they will have a period of months – six if the examination is at Easter, ten if it is in November – between passing the qualifying examination and entering the university. The fear is that, having attained their objective, they will sit back and do nothing but lose the habit of systematic and strenuous study.

My answer to the first objection is that all that is required to

[1] *Report of an* ad hoc *Committee on Procedure for Admission of Students*, Committee of Vice-Chancellors and Principals of the Universities of the United Kingdom, 1958.

meet it is a slight adjustment of the standard required for an examination pass, or a slight pruning of syllabuses. My answer to the second is that for many of these youngsters a fallow period would be the best thing in the world, and that if the schools cannot find them an abundance of interesting things to do they do not know their job. Those few months could be an invaluable period for pursuing already established interests, and discovering new ones.

A solution to this problem must be found. I return to the theme I have touched upon several times already in this book; that the nation is investing large sums of money in university education for its ablest young minds, and, quite apart from the question of justice to the young people themselves, which must never be forgotten, it is entitled to be assured that the money is being wisely and economically used. And so long as the annual 'mad scramble' for university places goes on, injustice will be done to young people, some not inconsiderable amount of the nation's money will be wasted, and some ability will go without the training that would more adequately equip it for adult service.

Able minds are being denied university education because of hurried and unsystematic admission procedures. And possibly because of another reason. An increasing number of teachers, both school and university, are beginning to doubt seriously whether success in Advanced level G.C.E. examinations is the best criterion for judging potential ability. Professor R. A. C. Oliver, Professor of Education at Manchester University, is one of the foremost critics. 'A pre-war examination operating in a post-war situation', was how he described[1] the G.C.E. to the Home Universities conference in 1958; and he went on to suggest that the A level examination papers were a test of memorised information rather than of ability to think.

There is much truth in the criticism. Professor Oliver's proposed remedy was an examination at 'two levels, related to second-year sixth form standards attainable in two or three subjects of specialisation, the other to standards in a candidate's

[1] As reported in *The Times Educational Supplement*, December 19th, 1958.

other sixth form studies'.[1] This would almost certainly improve matters, but would not go to the root of the problem. All testing by written examinations of study limited to prescribed syllabuses, especially when success offers coveted prizes, tends to encourage cramming – or, if that word be thought objectionable, instruction by dictated notes and other means of giving pre-digested information. I am not suggesting that much of this takes place in English secondary schools; I have far too much respect for sixth-form teachers, many of whom do a magnificent job, often in adverse circumstances. But it does happen, and one result is that every year some students enter the university because of their teachers' ability rather than their own. Another, more frequent, is that students come up with their minds blunted and their enthusiasm dulled. Because of this, some of them swell the ranks of university failures.

More radical remedies than revision of the qualifying examinations which have been suggested include more interviewing of applicants; a system of 'accrediting', that is, accepting without examination candidates from schools approved for the purpose, such as has been tried in New Zealand; the use of a battery of standardised tests similar in design to those used by War Office Selection Boards, and later by the Civil Service Commissioners; and either a propaedeutic year before entry into the university, or a diagnostic year within it before proceeding to the degree course proper.

More interviewing could be done if there were more time, but the psychologists assure us with one voice that the short interview is a most unreliable prognostic instrument. A searching oral examination would give far surer results, but would take even more time. The 'accrediting' system, whereby candidates are accepted on the recommendation of the secondary school head, has been shown in New Zealand to produce sound results, but it still leaves the pupils in the non-accredited schools, which may be expected to have a larger proportion of doubtful candidates, to be tested by the conventional methods.[2] The W.O.S.B. and C.S.S.B.

[1] Ibid.
[2] See G. W. Parkyn, *Success and Failure at the University*, Vol. I, Oxford University Press, 1959.

'House Party' is an expensive and time-consuming method, but although doubts about some of the procedures and tests used have been expressed by some psychologists, it does appear to have produced on the whole good results. The introduction of either a propaedeutic or a diagnostic year raises very large questions of finance, staff, and accommodation, but that the diagnostic year is not altogether outside the range of practical politics seems to be shown by the fact that the one large-scale experiment in university education which has been undertaken in Britain since 1945, the University College of North Staffordshire, at Keele, includes this element. Admittedly, the 'Foundation Year' of general studies which all students must take before proceeding to degree courses, is intended to serve a quite different purpose: to give students a broadly-based course of general education before they proceed to more specialised studies. But it does allow a whole year in which students' abilities, aptitudes and interests can be observed in a university atmosphere; and it should surely be possible during such a year to assess potential very accurately.

It has to be remembered in considering the practicability of more elaborate entry tests that it is only to the applicants about whose ability to undertake university studies there is doubt that they need be applied; there are many candidates whose ability is so obvious as to render such tests unnecessary. It is the problem of the eleven-plus 'Border Zone' over again. But the eleven-plus testing machinery, though at its best far and away the most accurate predictor of ability in use in our country,[1] has nevertheless shown that, to be absolutely fair to all the examinees producing results in the middle reaches, the Border Zone must be broad; it should adequately cover the 'margin of error' of the measuring instrument. Research has suggested[2] that about 12 per cent of eleven-plus examinees are each year wrongly placed; this would imply that at least 15 per cent should be regarded as within the Border Zone. The percentage might well have to be greater in the

[1] By 'machinery' is meant here not only the standardised tests used, but these along with teachers' assessments.

[2] See *Admission to Grammar Schools*, by Alfred Yates and D. A. Pidgeon, Newnes Educational Co., 1957, pp. 144 *et seq.*

case of university entry; certainly it should be during the early years in which new testing procedures were being tried out.

Revision of the methods used for selecting university students would inevitably raise again the question of academic standards, which has been often, and anxiously, discussed during the post-war years. The U.G.C. has repeatedly expressed the view that the increase in the number of students should not involve any decline in the standards reached by students in their university studies. But, as the Vice-Chancellor of Manchester University, Professor W. Mansfield Cooper, said in 1959: 'If you insist at the point of entry on our dealing with more heterogeneous material, then you must be ready to face changes also at the point of departure'.[1]

The principal change so far noted in students' academic performance at the university appears to be that the greatly increased number of students – which implies the extension of opportunity to a vast pool of hitherto untapped ability – while it has produced no proportionate increase in the number of first class degrees, has produced a reduction in the proportion of poor degrees (whether honours or pass) and a large increase in the proportion of second class degrees. Fears have also been expressed that the proportion of students relegated during their university career from honours to pass or general degree courses has increased (but I know of no statistics confirming these fears), and that the proportion of failures, both during and at the end of the under-graduate course, has also increased.

Several sample investigations into the percentage of university failures have been made during recent years. In 1955 the Dean of the Faculty of Arts at Glasgow University stated[2] that in the academic year 1954-5 10 per cent of the students entering that Faculty had failed to pass any degree examinations, though they had had two opportunities to do so, and that in the Science Faculty 11 per cent had similarly failed. Early in 1956 Professor F. A. Vick, then head of the Department of Physics at the

[1] As reported in *The Times*, May 14th, 1959.

[2] As reported in *The Times Educational Supplement*, December 25th, 1955.

University College of North Staffordshire, said[1] that a survey he had made of 1,300 students in the physics departments of five universities revealed that 22 per cent had failed to proceed to the second-year course. In the same year the University of Liverpool published a survey[2] covering 2,214 students in that University who embarked on first degree or first diploma or certificate courses in the three years 1947–9. Of that number 1,915, or 87·7 per cent, were ultimately successful, though only 71·1 per cent succeeded within the normal time. The remaining 12·3 per cent either withdrew, or had taken more than two years beyond the normal period to secure their degree, diploma or certificate.

In 1957 the Welsh Correspondent of *The Times Educational Supplement* reported[3] that in 1955–6 of 1,459 university students holding major awards from Welsh local education authorities who that year completed their course 275, or about 23 per cent, had either withdrawn or failed to pass their examinations.

The largest investigation made was by the U.G.C.[4] With the co-operation of all the universities they learned about 15,256 undergraduate students who were admitted in October 1952 to courses of three or four years in arts, pure science, and technology. By the end of the session 1955–6 80.6 per cent had successfully completed their course. Of the others 5.4 per cent had withdrawn for reasons other than academic failure, and 2.7 per cent had been re-admitted to continue their courses in the year 1956–7. Thus the percentage of failures was 11·3. It should be emphasised that this is an aggregate percentage, derived from returns from all the British universities. More detailed scrutiny would certainly reveal that failure rates vary from university to university, and probably even more between Faculty and Faculty and Department and Department. Even from the statistics I have recorded it will be

[1] As reported in *The Times Educational Supplement*, January 6th, 1956.

[2] *How they Fared*, by the Vice-Chancellor, Sir James Mountford, Liverpool University Press, 1956.

[3] *The Times Educational Supplement*, August 23rd, 1957.

[4] See *University Development* 1952–7, H.M.S.O., 1958, p. 21. A later enquiry showed only 9·9 per cent of failures.

seen that the rate given by Professor Vick is almost double the national rate, and that given by the Welsh Correspondent of *The Times Educational Supplement* (for grant-aided students only) more than double. On the other hand the *Oxford Magazine* in 1958 claimed, on the basis of returns from all the colleges,[1] that of 2,454 students who came up to Oxford in October 1957 only 96, or one in 26, was sent down or rusticated for failing to pass the examinations at the end of the first year. In only four colleges was the failure rate as high as one in 12. An enquiry made in Sheffield University in 1959 showed a total failure rate of only six per cent, and doubtless other universities could produce similarly low rates. But what would they mean ? There was much truth in the comment made by the *Schoolmaster* columnist Peter Quince in March 1959:[2]

> It is a pleasant academic conceit that a student in one university can be compared with a student in another, or that a degree in one faculty can be compared with a degree in another. But it is a conceit that has no real validity. It is like asking whether I can run a hundred yards better than you can paint a picture of Big Ben. The two things are not comparable.

By comparison with some other countries the failure rate in British universities is very low. When I was in Australia in 1950 I was told that at one university withdrawals and examination failures amounted to 40 per cent of the total number of students, and in the U.S.A. the failure rate is said to exceed 50 per cent in some universities. Too much must not be made of such comparisons; the stricter the selection the lower the failure rate should be, and selection for university entry in Britain is beyond question far stricter than in either America or Australia.

Low though it may be, the failure rate in Britain is high enough to cause concern, and to demand systematic investigation into its causes. These are known to be many and varied. According to Sir James Mountford[3] they include:

---

[1] As reported in *The Times*, November 6th, 1958.
[2] March 20th, 1959.
[3] In *How they Fared*, as summarised in *The Times Educational Supplement*, November 30th, 1956.

Amongst causes external to the university itself may be mentioned: unsuitable working conditions at home; frictions within the family; undue demands on the student for household chores; family financial worries; strain and waste of time in travelling too great a distance daily between home and university. In some cases there is a general lack of physical tone; in others there are emotional disturbances; and in the case of oversea students there are many problems arising from life in a strange environment. Some students are found to be taking a course simply because of parental pressure; others appear to have misjudged their aptitude for the subject they have chosen. Excess of zeal in the activities of student societies or in outside organisations proves to be the undoing of some, while a streak of sheer laziness brings disaster to others. In most instances, however, it is not really possible to put one's finger on a single cause.

To that list can be added many more items: indifferent, improper, or too exacting teaching at school or university; too little personal guidance at either or both; inadequate residential, refectory, lecture room, library, and laboratory accommodation at the university; inability to adapt to a very different educational environment; conflict of loyalties between home and university, particularly in the case of the many students who come from homes without previous contact with the Grammar school, let alone the University; a 'Welfare State' attitude of mind which regards a grant from public funds as a prize for being a bright boy rather than as an aid to serious and responsible study; over-indulgence during vacations in gainful employment unrelated to university activities; worry about a job at the end of the university career, and so on. And it must be remembered that such causes produce not only withdrawals and outright failures but also poorer *successful* results than should have been achieved. It may well be that these last are a matter for more serious concern than the relatively small proportion of students who become obvious failures.

Some of these matters I will discuss in the final chapter. I wish to conclude this with a special note about students from oversea, of whom there were in the British universities in 1958–9 over 10,000. Of these, more than 6,000 came from countries in the British Commonwealth, and of these a large number were coloured men and women. It is of them that I wish to speak.

To begin I cannot do better than quote some sentences from an article in the *Universities Review* of October 1958 written by Mr A. S. Livingstone, an Australian university teacher who had also been a United Nations consultant on education for social work in Pakistan.

> In many countries of Asia and Africa, the goal of attaining an overseas degree is something in the nature of an obsession, leading many to ignore, or depreciate, the value of similar studies that may have been developed in their own land. The belief that overseas training will confer on them prestige and opportunity for more rapid promotion is not without substance . . .

Even from that moderately-worded statement one can begin to appreciate the consequences of failure to secure the coveted overseas degree. And, unhappily, the circumstances predisposing to failure are more numerous and more difficult to overcome for oversea students, particularly coloured students, than for home students.

The coloured students can be divided into two categories: those who are sponsored by their governments or a responsible organisation in their country, and those who come on their own initiative. Many of the latter, and even some of the former are, in Mr Livingstone's words, 'ill-equipped to profit from training in Britain', because 'neither the nature of their previous studies nor the extent of their work experience at home prepares them for the opportunities offered here'.

Apart from the doubtful quality of their previous academic studies, many of them have an inadequate command of the English language. With some this is immediately obvious in conversation; others are fluent enough in everyday small-talk, but unable to understand thoroughly their lectures and textbooks. Add to that the grave difficulties of social adjustment and – again I quote Mr Livingstone – 'the debilitating effects of such factors as restrictive accommodation, unfamiliar food, harsh weather, loneliness . . .'

Home-born British university students are, I believe, invariably friendly to coloured students, and do their best to be helpful. The same is true of members of staff, whether academic, administrative, or domestic. Landladies vary; most of those prepared to lodge oversea students (not all will) are friendly and helpful. But, inevitably, many people in all these groups cannot even dimly understand some of the oversea students' problems; only persons with long experience of the countries concerned could do that.

The British Council, to which is delegated much responsibility for oversea students' welfare, does admirable work within the narrow limits of its resources. The Embassies and High Commissions for the countries concerned maintain oversight of the interests of their own nationals, some of them excellently. The Commonwealth Relations Office and the Colonial Office play their parts. Voluntary organisations do valuable work. But, with the best will in the world, little of all the effort expended by these bodies can really affect the coloured student's daily struggle with living, language, and study. And only radically improved methods of preparing him for study in Britain, and for looking after his welfare while he is in our country, can ease those struggles for him. I do not pretend to know the answer to this problem, but I will repeat one suggestion I have frequently made elsewhere: that all students whose mother tongue is not English should live in Britain, under expert and understanding care, for at least three months before they begin their studies. I am told that there is no money for this. Why not? These young people will many of them be the leaders of their countries in the future, facing problems of a magnitude and difficulty we can scarcely conceive in our mature, stable, and wealthy society. Only a few score thousands of pounds a year would do what I suggest. I believe the effect would be enormously beneficial. Could we not at least try it?

I have stated the case here in baldest outline. Interested readers are referred, not only to the article from which I have quoted, but also to the study, *Colonial Students in Britain*, published by P.E.P. (Political and Economic Planning, 16, Queen Anne's Gate, London, S.W.1) in 1955.

CHAPTER FIVE

How far are the Universities of Great Britain at present in a position to offer their students all that a University education ought to imply? Of all possible questions concerning Universities this is the most fundamental and the one which must most constantly engage the attention of University teachers and administrators. – UNIVERSITY GRANTS COMMITTEE.[1]

The question put by the U.G.C. over twenty years ago is as pertinent now as it was then. It has an even greater importance today, because the massive expansion which is taking place is giving the universities not only a much changed but also a far more responsible and incalculably more valuable role to play in the nation's life.

It is embarrassing to put the question today, because the universities are working under a strain more tense than any they have experienced for centuries, and are facing a much wider range of more formidable problems than they have ever known before. The past fifteen years have allowed them little opportunity for fundamental thought about aims and objectives. But during that period the universities have grown into one of the nation's largest enterprises and one of its most vitally important. It is therefore essential that it shall be asked, and asked persistently. The British universities have today entrusted to their care the higher education of over 100,000 of the nation's ablest young minds, and within a few years may have charge of double that number. No effort must be spared to ensure that the job is supremely well done.

Some of the observations made in this chapter will be critical of aspects of university work. I wish to preface them by paying unstinted tribute to the thousands of men and women, in all kinds

[1] *Report for the period 1929–30 to 1934–5*, H.M.S.O., 1936, p. 11.

and grades of university service, who are faithfully performing their various tasks – and often doing much more than is required of them – loyally, devotedly, and, if I may say so without seeming to appear patronising, with very great intelligence and initiative. I have during the past fifteen years paid visits, short but intensive in most cases, to all the universities in the United Kingdom, and have had the privilege of working in one for five years. I would ask to be believed when I say that this tribute is no mere lip-service, but an honest assessment arrived at from first-hand experience. I would like to add also a more personal note: that while I have been at the University of Sheffield I have been the recipient of innumerable spontaneous gestures of friendship and acts of helpfulness from my colleagues – again, in all parts of the University's service – and that these, together with similar gestures and acts from the training colleges, schools, local education authorities, and voluntary organisations in the Institute of Education's area, have made my years there among the happiest in my life.

My first criticism is not of the universities but of the British Government – every Government since the war. None has thought in financial terms sufficiently large to match the expansions each has piled upon the universities. Admittedly, since February 1958, when the then Government announced a provisional university building programme of £60,000,000 over the four years 1960–3, some approach to realisation seems to have dawned of the capital cost of doubling or trebling the university population and demanding of the universities that they supply the great bulk of professional men and women. But even today the financial provision being made by the State is grossly inadequate to enable the universities to do a first-rate job. As things are, they, like the schools, whose cost has been similarly underestimated, are doing a far better job than the circumstances often warrant, but that is no excuse for continued parsimony. No Government can by now plead ignorance of the need for greatly increased subventions; the evidence is overwhelmingly conclusive.

Until this matter is put right the universities cannot be 'in a position to offer their students all that a university education ought to imply'. And to put it right means something like doubling the present annual amounts for recurrent expenditure, with *pro rata* increases as student numbers grow. About capital expenditure it is not possible to be precise, because not only money but man-power and materials are involved. All I can say is: as great an increase in non-recurrent grants as can be used. The universities cannot give their best until they have a reasonable range of build-ings in which to work, and sufficient equipment to make it pos-sible for them to do their work well. I include under this head, in addition to teaching premises, the adequate residential ac-commodation for which I have pleaded, and provisions for social and recreative activities.

My first criticism of the universities, and the U.G.C. must be associated with them in this, is that they have not done anything like sufficient experiment, either large- or small-scale, with new means and methods of university work. The only large-scale experiment since the war is the University College of North Staffordshire at Keele, unless one includes the acceptance by the universities of responsibility for the academic side of all teacher training, and their consequent establishment of University Insti-tutes of Education. Keele has enough unique features to keep half-a-dozen institutions busy. It is completely residential, for both staff and students; it stands in an enclosed, and isolated, estate; it has a four-year undergraduate course, compulsory for all students, of which the first year is quite unlike any other in the United Kingdom, while the degree course proper not only pre-cludes the intense specialisation common to almost all honours degrees in the other universities, but compels all students to read in both the humanities and the sciences; and those of its under-graduates intending to be teachers do a concurrent course of academic study and professional training instead of doing the latter after the former, as is the invariable practice in all the other English universities.

No praise can be too high for the courage, initiative and imagination which conceived and launched the University College of North Staffordshire. But why has it not been followed by other foundations incorporating some of its unique features, perhaps with variations, or adding new ones ? I am told that the University of Sussex is to include some experimental features; but this is not expected to open until, at earliest, 1961. One large-scale experiment every eleven years is hardly enough to meet the challenge of the age of social revolution in which we are living.

That there have been many small-scale experiments I do not deny. But some of the more obvious fields for experiment appear, at least to the outside observer, to have remained untouched. No two academic problems have been more discussed, or with a greater sense of urgency, than intensive specialisation and the necessity of ensuring that scientists are not unacquainted with the humanities and students of humane subjects with the sciences. But, apart from those at Keele, how many university courses specifically designed to resolve one or other of these problems have been started since 1945 ? A few, but I venture to say not nearly enough. I doubt whether anyone would claim that the universities have seriously attempted to get to grips with either problem.

To turn, by way of example only, to another kind of problem. In the *Observer* of December 20th, 1959 Mr John Davy, the paper's Science Correspondent, pointed out that:

> Future research workers and future science teachers take identical science degrees. Yet research is an utterly different activity from teaching, and the laboratory a different world from the classroom.

Mr Davy maintained that:

> Present science degrees are designed to train research workers. They are ludicrously lop-sided and unsuitable as a preparation for teaching.

To what extent that is correct I am not competent to say; I am not a scientist. Mr Davy was presumably referring only to degrees in pure science; his statement is certainly not applicable to all degrees in applied science. Speaking generally, I would not be prepared to push very far, if at all, the argument for *ad hoc* degrees within the university. This particular problem seems to me to fall within the category of those best solved by the diversion, which I have earlier suggested, of some students, for either the whole or part of their advanced education, from the university to other, more specialised institutions of higher learning, which could (and in fact do) offer courses leading to appropriate awards, specifically tailored to meet the needs of individual occupations. The university could then concentrate upon the academic disciplines which are its primary concern.

Concentration upon academic disciplines might do something to ease a problem which obsesses multitudes of students: the swollen syllabuses which, they claim, prevent their pursuit of other intellectual interests, or even much participation in social and athletic activities. I must confess that I would be much more impressed by this complaint did I not hear from so many students (not by any means all at Sheffield University) of their long weeks spent during vacations in gainful employment completely unrelated to any academic (or even mental) activity. No one would wish to bar students from doing a moderate amount of wage-earning work between terms; their grants, or allowances from their parents, often do not permit of much expenditure on anything except sheer necessities. But even the longest university terms in England leave over four months' vacation a year, surely enough time in which both to earn some pocket-money and to do several weeks of steady reading? A university education today is much too costly, and its success too crucially important, to both the student and to this country, to permit of its being regarded as a part-time occupation.

It cannot be too strongly emphasised that the overriding purpose of a university education is academic study. Any activity which interrupts or lowers the quality of this study is defeating the purpose. One minor, but nevertheless serious, cause of interruption of some students' academic studies is over-long concentration on preparations for 'Rag Day', or, as it it has become in some places, 'Rag Week'. The case of the student who admitted[1] to having missed 'possibly as many as 45 per cent' of lectures

[1] As quoted in *The Times*, February 9th, 1959.

one term in order to help with the organisation of the university rag week may be an extreme one, but there is no doubt that every year a number of students spend a disproportionate amount of time on rag activities. Nor is that the sum total of the trouble; in recent years some 'rags' appear to have got completely out of hand; it is gratifying to note that in 1959 the authorities of at least five British universities took action about 'rag' rowdyism and damage to property.

But the fact that many students devote their vacations to gainful employment, and a few waste time during term on extraneous activities, is no answer to the problem of overloaded syllabuses, which afflicts also many conscientious and hard-working students, and is a matter of deep concern to their teachers. The root cause of this problem is the perpetual accretion of new knowledge, more particularly in the pure and applied sciences. There are several possible remedies. The first, and most obvious, is a severe, and continuous, pruning of syllabuses. A second is the lowering of the ceiling of attainment (not the *standard*, which is a matter of quality) required for a first degree. A third is the lengthening of the time allowed for the undergraduate course. There are objections made to all these measures; but to allow the syllabuses to continue to expand is to court a progressive deterioration in the quality of both learning and teaching in the university.

An enquiry into this problem might well be part of a larger enquiry covering the entire range of university learning and teaching. Such an enquiry seems to me to be urgently needed, in the interests of both students and teachers.

In 1958 I was criticised by some academics (but applauded by more) for making adverse comments about university teachers and teaching methods, in an article published in the *Observer* on October 12th. I was able to point out to my critics that the comments to which they most objected only expressed in blunter language what the U.G.C. said in their quinquennial report on the years 1952-7, which was published a few days before my article. Nevertheless, the critics had a case. Within the narrow confines of a newspaper article it is impossible to include the qualifications and reservations one would wish to add to almost every positive statement made, and which, if one is to be fair to those whom one criticises, must be made. There is no excuse for not including these in the ampler framework of a book.

I said, first, that 'Few university staff are trained teachers'. That is true, though I think there is no doubt that the proportion which has received professional training for teaching is increasing, probably fairly rapidly. What I had not space to add was a description of the kind of training I would consider helpful. That omission not unnaturally caused some misunderstanding. I had no intention of implying that I thought it desirable for all university teachers to undergo such a course as is given in a training college or university department of education. For men and women intending to devote themselves entirely to university work, either, in its present form, would be inappropriate. What I had in mind was that anyone appointed to a university academic staff for the first time, without previous experience of teaching, and particularly if young, would be better equipped for the job if he or she had had some instruction in the arts of lecturing and handling seminar and tutorial groups, in preparing lecture notes, summaries, and scripts, in the psychology of learning and of later adolescence, the general structure of the English educational system with particular reference to the university, and at least the rudiments of knowledge about one or two other national systems of education.

My second comment, that many university teachers, 'especially among the younger, resent having to teach at all', because 'they regard research as their primary function, and teaching as an annoying interruption of it', produced three different kinds of reply: first, that it was perfectly true; secondly, that it was not true; and thirdly, that some teachers had such heavy teaching loads that they had no time for research, and that that was what they resented, not the fact of having to teach.

If the word 'many' be interpreted (as it was by some people) as meaning the majority of university teachers I was undoubtedly guilty of exaggeration. But if, as I intended, 'many' be taken to mean 'not few', I know the statement to be true, having heard it expressed by so many people better qualified to judge than I, including people who made no secret of the fact that they objected to having to teach. Even had I not, I still had the evidence of the U.G.C., recorded in its Report on the years 1952-7, that:[1]

> ... we were told in one university that members of staff should be relieved so far as possible from the 'distraction' of teaching and administrative duties (bracketed together as drudgery) so that they can make progress with their work, which they identify with their research.

and that, in the Committee's opinion:

> In some departments in some universities the pendulum has swung too far [i.e., from Jowett of Balliol's view that 'education, not research, is the first and the final function of a tutor']. University students include the cream of each generation . . . To teach them is a high responsibility, and we think that it would be salutary for every university teacher who seeks relief from teaching to ask himself whether it is really the call of duty which prompts him to do so.

My own comment, that this attitude would not change until universities ceased 'to appoint, and promote, almost exclusively upon the evidence of papers published in learned journals' was not, apparently, disputed. I did not expect it to be, knowing how deep and widespread is the feeling of resentment among junior staff about the current emphasis on 'publications'. I shall return to this matter later.

The sentences in my *Observer* article which provoked the greatest volume of hostile criticism were those which asserted that 'many lecturers are, as teachers, under-employed. Four to six lectures a week during three terms of eight to ten weeks can hardly be called onerous, even allowing for research'. My critics, with considerable justification, interpreted these sentences, which I admit were maladroitly worded, to mean that I was implying that the *average* stint of a university lecturer is 'four to six lectures a week'. No idea was further from my mind. I am sadly aware, and was when I wrote the article, that this is far from being the

[1] *University Development* 1952-7, p. 43, paras. 83 and 84.

average, that there are unfortunate lecturers, especially perhaps in applied science departments, who have as much as 18 hours a week of formal teaching, and on top of that marking of laboratory reports and supervision of experimental work and theses; and that the *average* number of teaching hours for a lecturer in such departments may well be twelve or more, and in other departments up to double the figures I gave. I greatly regret the pain I gave to many people by wording those sentences in such a way as to leave them wide open to misinterpretation. Nevertheless, my statements, taken absolutely and not relatively, are correct. Again I call the latest report of the U.G.C. in evidence.[1] In paragraph 53 on page 30 the Committee state that:

... There has been a further increase in the staff/student ratio [that is, as stated in a footnote, 'for institutions other than Cambridge and Oxford'] to 1 to 7·2 in 1956–7. This further improvement is to be welcomed; it will, however, be appreciated that the ratios quoted are averages covering very wide variations between one subject and another, and that in so far as additional appointments are due to the growing needs of research and the increased specialisation which becomes necessary as the volume of knowledge increases, the beneficial effect on undergraduate teaching is less than might appear.

And further, in paragraph 66, page 35, that:

... the overall ratio of 1 to 7·2 conceals wide variations between one department and another, and there must be a number of cases in which teaching loads are light enough to enable members of staff to give generous time to study and research even during full term.

If, as is undoubtedly the case, there are many university teachers with teaching loads amounting to 12, 14, 16, and 18 hours a week, it seems clear that there must also be a considerable number where the load is six hours or less. There may be perfectly good reasons for such light loads; I am not questioning that, but simply stating the facts.

[1] *University Development*, 1952–7.

These facts ought in my opinion to be made the subject of authoritative scrutiny, because there are few more important questions in academic life than that of the respective places of research and teaching in a university teacher's work. As is well known, this question, far from being a new one, has been debated for centuries, and quotations I have given earlier in this book show how completely eminent university teachers have disagreed about it. I give my own opinion not merely for the purpose of clarifying a published statement which, owing to its brevity, may have caused unnecessary irritation, but also because I feel that it is urgently necessary today to use the services of every university teacher to the very best advantage. That is not possible so long as the claims of research and teaching are regarded as conflicting. I believe that every member of the academic staff of a university should be constantly engaged in research, but not necessarily, nor perhaps even usually, with the idea of immediate or early publication. He should be exploring some of the frontiers of knowledge in his subject, for his own intellectual refreshment, and in order, as the U.G.C. put it in 1930,[1] 'to fertilise his teaching of students'. If a member of staff proves capable of doing research which may lead to original discoveries I hold it to be entirely proper to appoint or promote him to a post involving light teaching duties only, or in exceptional cases carrying no regular teaching duties at all. I believe that every university should have the power to create such posts, over and above the Research Fellowships which every university has. But, as the U.G.C., who return to this topic again and again in their Reports, wrote in 1936:[2]

The number of persons who are capable of the pioneering discoveries which definitely advance the frontiers of knowledge is limited . . . On the other hand, the number who are capable of delving into some abstruse but not necessarily very significant aspect of learning is considerable, and we think it would be

[1] *Report including Returns from Universities and University Colleges in Receipt of Treasury Grant, Academic Year* 1928–9, H.M.S.O., 1930, p. 34.

[2] University Grants Committee. *Report for the period* 1929–30 *to* 1934–5, p. 43.

singularly unfortunate if research of this latter character, of which perhaps there is already too much being done all over the world, were to be rewarded in preference to work which bears fruit, not in an accumulation of publications, but in the inspiration of teaching.

I agree entirely with that statement. In my opinion, the primary duty of most university teachers today is to teach, and to teach as well as possible. That they can only do if they themselves are continuously students, enriching their knowledge and understanding of their subject by constant reading at a high level. The object of their research is the betterment of themselves as scholars and as teachers; whether or not papers in learned journals, or books, result is a secondary consideration. If they find they have something to tell the world, it is their duty to tell it; and in fact nothing will stop them from doing so. But if not, they can still be first-rate scholars and teachers.

The wise distribution of a university's resources depends upon those bodies and individuals to whom it entrusts its government and administration. There are three different types of government to be found among the universities of England and Wales. At Oxford and Cambridge the principal governing bodies consist entirely of members of the academic and administrative staff; and the colleges, all of which possess a large measure of autonomy, are similarly self-governed. The numerous institutions which make up the University of London also enjoy a considerable degree of autonomy, though not so large as that of the Oxbridge colleges. Their governing bodies include lay members, and so do the principal governing bodies of the University: the Court, which controls the finances, and the Senate, which controls all other university matters. The governmental machinery at the provincial universities consists essentially (with variations in detail) of three bodies: the Court, a large body containing a majority of lay members; the Council, a much smaller body in which lay members are also in the majority; and the Senate, which is composed entirely of members of the academic and senior administrative staff. Constitutionally, the Court is the supreme organ of government, but ordinarily it meets only once a year, and its acts are largely formal. The chief executive body is the Council. The Senate is responsible for all academic matters, though as a rule senior appointments to the academic staff have to be confirmed by Council. The details of academic work are arranged and supervised by the Faculties, which report to the Senate.

University government, like any other form of government, has been criticised ever since it began; and it always will be. I feel that it would be extraordinarily unwise to attempt, at the present time, any major alteration in the structure of any of the three types of government; the upheaval would be enormous, the advantages problematic. My criticisms are therefore, with one exception, directed at parts of the machinery within the structure; and they have reference only to the Redbrick universities.

In these universities the influence in government of lay participation has recurrently been a bone of contention; I hold it to be exceedingly valuable, but feel that it need not today and in the future play so dominating a part as it has done in some universities in the past. As regards internal regulation of academic matters I agree entirely with Sir Eric Ashby[1] that the practice whereby all business flows upwards is both sound and democratic; but I am very doubtful whether so much of it need necessarily have to flow through so many channels. There are moments when one coming newly to the conduct of academic affairs in a university wonders whether its procedures are not specifically designed to prevent anything happening quickly. The number of academic committees, standing and *ad hoc*, is truly formidable; again, one wonders how some of the more experienced professors, upon whom every university relies so heavily, ever manage to escape from the committee room into their departments. Somehow, some do, and somehow, they manage to be an inspiration and guiding force in both places. But the feat seems to me little short of miraculous. They should not be required to carry such a heavy load of administration; some of these men are worth their weight in gold as scholars, and scholarship should be their prime concern.

[1] See *Technology and the Academics*, Chap. 5.

The most crushing weight of all falls upon the Vice-Chancellor. That load should at all costs be lightened, for the sake of the man, and because if ever universities needed clear-headed and vigorous leadership it is today; and it will be more so tomorrow, when numbers will be greater and problems of policy no less. A friend of mine thinks that the Vice-Chancellor should have a 'Cabinet' of senior university officers, academic and administrative, and be able to delegate to them and others the chairmanship of all but the most important university committees. I applaud both ideas.

Participation in academic government by members of the non-professorial staff, about which a stern and prolonged struggle was waged during the inter-war years, is still, I think, inadequate, especially in Senate and Council. But increased representation in Senate would exacerbate an already embarrassing problem. Even in the medium-sized British universities Senate is becoming an unwieldy body with a membership too large to permit full discussion. At Sheffield, for example, in 1960, when the student population was only 2,800, Senate was already over 50 strong; and in only slightly larger universities, I was told, it ran to 80 or more. Whether all the business that comes up to Senate from the Faculties need necessarily do so I do not feel competent to judge; but some people more entitled to an opinion than I think not. Some even query whether the present organisation of the University into Faculties is the best for present-day circumstances. But that is a very large and complex question.

About the supremely important matters of university autonomy and freedom many millions of words have been spoken and written, and doubtless many more will be. I do not propose to add much here to what I have said earlier.

I have tried in these pages to show how the English universities early rid themselves of control by local authorities, and how after long centuries they were finally freed from the ecclesiastical control under which they started, but that they never freed themselves from a measure of State control. Nor, indeed, does it appear to me that the older universities ever seriously attempted to do so; and the modern university colleges, as soon as they were in serious financial difficulties, turned, as if it were the natural thing to do, to the State for aid. And this, after a not unreasonable period of time, they received. For long, it is true, on conditions which seriously handicapped their development; until 1945 they were regarded, and treated, as recipients of State charity, not as partners in a national enterprise. But that is now unquestionably their status, and consequently it is today a contradiction in terms to talk of the universities as being 'independent of the State'. They are part of it.

What seems to me to be absolutely essential is to distinguish clearly between political independence and academic freedom, between the University as an institution in and of society and the methods by which that institution performs its particular and unique task. Political independence of the State the British universities no longer possess – if ever they did, which my reading of history inclines me to doubt. What they do possess is a very substantial measure of autonomy. Their present position *vis*-à-*vis* the State has, I think, been accurately summarised by an American writer, Mr Robert O. Berdahl:[1]

> The state has a legitimate interest in the over-all policies of the universities, whether these are public or private institutions and whether or not public funds are involved. The universities should form their educational policies with sensitivity for national needs, and, if subsidized by public funds, after consultation with the appropriate governmental offices. In case of disagreement over ends or means between the state and the universities, the universities' judgment should prevail, with the understanding that they have the responsibility of demonstrating the wisdom of their decisions within a reasonable time, and subject always to ultimate intervention in the face of a major breakdown in higher education. The execution of the subsidized policies should be entirely free from the close state supervision which normally accompanies grants of public funds. And, finally, the state organ which links the universities to the government should be composed primarily, but not exclusively,

[1] In *British Universities and the State*, Cambridge University Press, 1959, p. 193.

of university men who are not only thoroughly familiar with the work and ideals of the universities but also cognizant of the state's broader domestic problems and external responsibilities.

The academic freedom of the universities is as inviolate as ever: more so, in my opinion. But of what does that freedom consist? Sir Hector Hetherington, Vice-Chancellor and Principal of Glasgow University, some years ago declared[1] that:

I think it vital that the Universities should each retain full responsibility for its own appointments: that it alone, subject to the ordinary law of the land, should choose its teachers, should settle the conditions of their tenure, and should, if need be, dismiss them. That is the primary condition of University freedom, and the only ground of assurance that its members may speak and teach in whatever way they are responsibly led to do . . . And the corollary is that the University must retain full responsibility for the organisation of its courses, and for the character and standards of the instruction given within its walls.

Those rights the British universities possess. They are not disputed by anyone. But I am sure that it is necessary to include others. The university should have absolute control over the admission, examination, and expulsion of students. It should have, subject to any agreements freely negotiated with other bodies, the absolute right to determine what forms of research, and what research projects, it will as a corporate body undertake, or approve for individuals working under its official direction. It should have the final voice in the distribution of public funds received for purposes of recurrent expenditure, including the right to divert sums – provided good cause can be shown – from one purpose to another. I believe it should have the same right of diversion in respect of projects involving only minor capital expenditure. Major capital expenditure is another matter;

[1] In the P. J. Anderson Memorial Lecture, 1954. Aberdeen University Studies, No. 133, p. 10.

building projects involving very large sums must be subject to final decisions.

Not all these rights are uncontested; in particular, as has been shown earlier, some aspects of financial control by the university have been called in question; and I doubt whether those I have suggested above would command universal acceptance. But I hold them to be necessary if the university is to be enabled to undertake freely, imaginatively, and flexibly its unique task.

This task is not merely to purvey information and conduct research. It is also to nurture the ablest minds of each generation. And so, finally, I return to Sir Walter Moberly's accusation[1] that 'Broadly speaking, the university today is not asking the really fundamental questions', and is neglecting its moral duty by allowing most of its students to spend the whole of their time within its walls 'without ever having been forced to exercise their minds on the issues which are really momentous'.

This accusation raises the ultimate question: is it, as Sir Charles Grant Robertson has suggested, the duty of the university to be 'the starting point of a new renaissance' whose purpose is 'to raise spiritual and moral power'? Some would deny it; but I believe that it is. That belief is at the heart of my plea for ensuring that the university shall remain a community, whose members, young and old, can live together and play together and wrestle with the fundamental problems of life together, as well as pursue their intellectual tasks together. Spiritual and moral power can be generated to the full only through complete living: and I hold it to be the duty of the university to lead its members towards that ideal. Those who pass through the university will in any case largely determine in later life the nation's standards: they should have every opportunity to learn how to set and keep them high.

[1] In *The Crisis in the University*.

SELECT BIBLIOGRAPHY

GENERAL WORKS

Armytage, W. H. G., *Civic Universities*, Benn, 1955.

Ashby, Sir Eric, *Technology and the Academics*, Macmillan, 1958.

Barker, Sir Ernest, *Universities in Great Britain*, S C M Press, 1931; *British Universities*, Longmans, for the British Council, 1946.

Berdahl, Robert O., *British Universities and the State*, C.U.P., 1959.

Cardwell, D. S. L., *The Organisation of Science in England*, Heinemann, 1957.

Dent, H. C., *Education in Transition*, 5th Ed., Routledge, 1948; *Growth in English Education, 1946–52*, Routledge, 1954.

Flexner, A., *Universities, American, English, German*, Clarendon Press, 1930.

Gasset, José Ortega y, tr. Howard Lee Nostrand, *Mission of the University*, Routledge, 1944.

Glass, D. V. (Ed.), *Social Mobility in Britain*, Routledge, 1954.

Herklots, H. G. G., *The New Universities*, Benn, 1928.

Kneller, George F., *Higher Learning in Britain*, C.U.P., 1955.

Leach, A. F., *Educational Charters and Documents 598–1909*, C.U.P., 1911; *The Schools of Medieval England*, Methuen, 1915.

Livingstone, Sir Richard, *Some Thoughts on University Education*, C.U.P., 1948; *The Rainbow Bridge*, Pall Mall Press, 1959.

Löwe, Adolf, *Universities in Transformation*, Sheldon Press, 1940.

Moberly, Sir Walter, *The Crisis in the University*, S C M Press, 1949.

Nash, Arnold S., *The University and the Modern World*, S C M Press, 1945.

Newman, J. H., ed. McHugh, Roger J., *On the Scope and Nature of University Education*, Browne & Nolan, 1944.

Nuffield College, *The Problem facing British Universities*, O.U.P., 1948.

Parker, Irene, *Dissenting Academies in England*, C.U.P., 1914.

Parkyn, G. W., *Success and Failure at the University*, Vol. I, O.U.P., 1959.

Rait, R. S., *Life in the Mediaeval University*, C.U.P., 1912.

Rashdall, H., *Universities of Europe in the Middle Ages*, ed. F. M. Powicke and A. B. Emden, Clarendon Press, 1936.

Roberts, S. C., *British Universities*, Collins, 1947.

Robertson, Sir Charles Grant, *The British Universities*, Methuen, rev. ed., 1944.

Smith, Adam, *The Wealth of Nations*, Routledge, 1890.

Tillyard, A. I., *A History of University Reform from 1800 A.D. to the Present Time*, Heffer, 1913.

Trevelyan, G. M., *English Social History*, Longmans, 1944; *Shortened History of England*, Penguin Books, 1959.

Truscot, Bruce, *Redbrick University*, Faber, 1943; *Redbrick and these Vital Days*, Faber, 1945.

Yates, Alfred, and Pidgeon, D. A., *Admission to Grammar Schools*, Newnes Educational Publishing Co., 1957.

The Association of Universities of the British Commonwealth, *Commonwealth Universities Yearbook 1959*, 36 Gordon Square, W.C.1, 1959.

Bereday, George Z. F. and Lauwerys, Joseph A. (Editors), *The Year Book of Education 1959. Higher Education*, Evans Bros, 1959.

HISTORIES OF INDIVIDUAL UNIVERSITIES

Vincent, E. W. and Hinton, P., *The University of Birmingham. Its History and Significance*, Cornish, 1947.

Cottle, B. and Sherborne, J. W., *The Life of a University* (Bristol), Arrowsmith, 1951.

Glover, T. R., *Cambridge Retrospect*, C.U.P., 1943.

Porter, H. C., *Reformation and Reaction in Tudor Cambridge*, C.U.P., 1958.

Whiting, C. E., *The University of Durham, 1832-1932*, Sheldon Press, 1932.

Shimmin, A. N., *The University of Leeds, the First Half Century*, C.U.P., 1954.

Simmons, Jack, *New University* (Leicester), Leicester University Press, 1958.

Hearnshaw, F. J. C., *History of King's College* (London), Harrap, 1931.

Bellot, H. H., *University College London, 1826-1926*, University of London Press, 1929.

Dunsheath, Percy, and Miller, Margaret, *Convocation in the University of London*, Athlone Press, 1958.

Charlton, H. B., *Portrait of a University* (Manchester), Manchester University Press, 1951.

Gallie, W. B., *A New University. A. D. Lindsay and the Keele Experiment*, Chatto & Windus, 1960.

Wood, A. C., *The History of the University College of Nottingham, 1881-1948*, Blackwell, 1954.

Mallet, Sir C. E., *The History of the University of Oxford*, O.U.P., Vols. I and II, 1924; Vol. III, 1927.

Maxwell Lyte, H. C., *History of the University of Oxford*, Macmillan, 1886.

Childs, W. M., *Making a University* (Reading), Dent, 1933.

Chapman, A. W., *The Story of a Modern University* (Sheffield), O.U.P., 1955.

Evans, Sir D. E., *The University of Wales*, A Historical Sketch, University of Wales Press, 1953.

GOVERNMENT PUBLICATIONS, 1889-1913

Treasury Minutes relating to Grants to University Colleges in Great Britain.

Reports of Committee on Grants to University Colleges in Great Britain, 1889-1902.

Reports of University Colleges Committee, 1904-05.

Reports of Advisory Committee to the Treasury on the Distribution of the Grant in aid of Colleges furnishing Education of a University Standard, 1907-13.

Reports of Inspectors appointed by the Treasury, 1896-1901, and by the Advisory Committee, 1907, to visit Colleges in receipt of Grant.

Reports from Universities and University Colleges to the Board of Education, 1906-14.

University Grants Committee Reports, 1919–1959

On the period 1919–20 to 1923–24. 1925.
On the period 1923–24 to 1928–29. 1930.
On the period 1929–30 to 1934–35. 1936.
University Development from 1935 to 1947. 1948.
University Development. Interim Report on the years 1947 to 1951. 1952.
University Development. Report on the years 1947 to 1952. 1953.
University Development. Interim Report on the years 1952 to 1956. 1957.
University Development 1952–1957. 1958.
Returns from University and University Colleges in receipt of Treasury Grant, 1919–20 to 1958–59. 1921–60.
A Note on Technology in Universities. 1950.
Halls of Residence. 1957.

Other Governmental Reports, 1944–60

Report of the Inter-Departmental Committee on Medical Schools ('Goodenough' Report). 1944.
Second Report of the Committee on Veterinary Education in Great Britain. 1944.
Teachers and Youth Leaders ('McNair' Report). 1944.
Teachers: Supply, Recruitment and Training. Report of the Advisory Council on Education in Scotland. 1944.
Higher Technological Education ('Percy' Report). 1945.
Final Report of the Inter-Departmental Committee on Dentistry ('Teviot' Report). 1945.
Agricultural Education in Scotland ('Alness' Report). 1945.
Scientific Manpower ('Barlow' Report). 1946.
Report of the Committee on the Study of Oriental, Slavonic, East European and African languages ('Scarbrough' Report). 1946.
Report of the Committee on Higher Agricultural Education in England and Wales ('Loveday' Report). 1946.
Report of the Committee on the Provision for Social and Economic Research ('Clapham' Report). 1946.
University Awards. Reports of a Working Party appointed by the Minister of Education. 1948.
The Future Development of Higher Technological Education. Report of the National Advisory Council on Education for Industry and Commerce. 1950.
Technical Education. Cmd. 9703. 1956.
Report of the Commonwealth Education Conference. 1959.
Annual Report of the Advisory Council on Scientific Policy, 1958–59. 1959.
Scientific and Engineering Manpower in Great Britain 1959. 1959.
15 to 18 ('Crowther' Report). Report of the Central Advisory Council for Education—England. Vol. I, 1959; Vol. II, 1960.
Grants to Students ('Anderson' Report). 1960. (All the foregoing Reports from H.M. Stationery Office.)

NON-GOVERNMENTAL REPORTS, 1943–1960

British Association, *Reports of the Committee on Post-war University Education,* 1943.

Parliamentary and Scientific Committee, *Scientific Research and the Universities in Post War Britain,* 1943.

Association of University Teachers, *Report on Policy for University Expansion,* 1944.

Royal Institute of British Architects, *Architectural Education,* 1946.

Committee of Vice-Chancellors and Principals, *A Note on University Policy and Finance in the Decennium 1947–56,* 1946.

Younghusband, Eileen, for the Carnegie United Kingdom Trust, *Employment and Training of Social Workers,* 1947.

Kelsall, R. K., for the Committee of Vice-Chancellors and Principals, *Report on an Inquiry into Applications for Admission to Universities,* 1957.

Committee of Vice-Chancellors and Principals, *Report of an* ad hoc *Committee on Procedure for Admission of Students,* 1958; *Second Report,* 1960.

BOOKLETS, PAMPHLETS AND ADDRESSES

Simon, Sir Ernest, *The Development of British Universities,* Longmans, 1944.

P.E.P., *University Courses,* Vol. XVI, No. 306 of PLANNING, 1949; *University Students. A Pilot Survey,* Vol. XVI, No. 310, 1950; *The Universities and Adult Education,* Vol. XVII, No. 328, 1951; *Choosing University Students,* Vol. XIX, No. 357, 1953; *The Keele Experiment,* Vol. XX, No. 372, 1954; *Background of the University Student,* Vol. XX, No. 373, 1954; *Students from the Colonies,* Vol. XX, No. 374, 1954.

Southampton University College, *Centenary Commemoration Booklet,* 1950.

Rowe, A. P., *Some impressions resulting from a visit to British Universities,* Hassell Press, Adelaide, 1951.

Hetherington, Sir Hector, *The British University System 1914–54,* Aberdeen University Studies, No. 133, 1954.

Bowden, B. V., *The development of technological education in Europe, America and England,* Institution of Production Engineers, 1956.

Thomson, Sir George, *The education of scientists and technologists, today and tomorrow,* The Arthur Mellows Memorial Trust, Peterborough, 1957.

Communist Party, *Higher Education in the Nuclear Age.* A Communist Plan. 16 King Street, W.C.2, 1959.

Socialist Commentary, *A Policy for Higher Education,* 5 Earnshaw Street, W.C.2, 1959.

National Union of Students, *The Selection and Financing of Students,* 3 Endsleigh Street, W.C.1, 1959.

Moodie, Graeme C., *The Universities: a Royal Commission?* Fabian Society, 1959.

Crow, Duncan, *Commonwealth Education. The United Kingdom Contribution.* Central Office of Information, 1959.

National Union of Teachers, *University Entrance. The Basic Facts.* Hamilton House, W.C.1, 1960.

£11.00

Circle Time

for Nursery, Reception and Key Stage 1 Children

With ideas for PSHE and Citizenship
for children 3-8 years old

Margaret Collins

1

Lucky Duck is more than a publishing house and training agency. George Robinson and Barbara Maines founded the company in the 1980's when they worked together as a head and psychologist developing innovative strategies to support challenging students.

They have an international reputation for their work on bullying, self-esteem, emotional literacy and many other subjects of interest to the world of education.

George and Barbara have set up a regular news-spot on the website. Twice yearly these items will be printed as a newsletter. If you would like to go on the mailing list to receive this then please contact us:

Lucky Duck Publishing Ltd. 3 Thorndale Mews, Clifton, Bristol, BS8 2HX, UK

Phone: 0044 (0)117 973 2881   e-mail newsletter@luckyduck.co.uk
Fax: 044 (0)117 973 1707   website www.luckyduck.co.uk

ISBN: 1 873942 53 2

www.luckyduck.co.uk

Printed in Great Britain by Antony Rowe Limited.